BEST AMERICAN CARD GAMES

BEST AMERICAN CARD GAMES

by David Duncan

foulsham

LONDON • NEW YORK • TORONTO • SYDNEY

foulsham

Yeovil Road, Slough, Berkshire SL1 4JH

ISBN 0–572–01542–9
Copyright © 1989 W. Foulsham and Co. Ltd.

All rights reserved.
The Copyright Act (1956) prohibits (subject to certain very limited exceptions) the making of copies of any copyright work or of a substantial part of such a work, including the making of copies by photocopying or similar process. Written permission to make a copy or copies must therefore normally be obtained from the publisher in advance. It is advisable to consult the publisher if in any doubt as to the legality of any copying which is to be undertaken.

Printed in Great Britain at St. Edmundsbury Press,
Bury St. Edmunds.

CONTENTS

INTRODUCTION	6
GIN RUMMY AND HOLLYWOOD GIN	7
CONTINENTAL RUMMY	21
FIVE HUNDRED	25
OH HELL	34
HEARTS, BLACK LADY and OMNIBUS HEARTS	39
KLABBERJASS	51
PINOCHLE	60
AUCTION PINOCHLE	73
SEVEN UP	85
AUCTION PITCH	91
EIGHTS	97
MICHIGAN	102
RED DOG	110
RUSSIAN BANK	114
POKER SOLITAIRE	122

INTRODUCTION

Some card games are just as popular in Britain as in the United States. So Bridge, Canasta and Poker are equally well known in both countries, and Pontoon is the same game as American Blackjack or Twenty-One. Euchre, though Pennsylvania Dutch in origin, has also reached a wide audience in this country. On the other hand there is additionally a whole range of games that command huge followings across the Atlantic but which are hardly ever played here. In most cases they are known only by repute, through the medium of American books and films. It is these games that this book is about.

They are presented here in the belief that card players in this country will welcome a full and accurate description of games whose merits have made them favourites in the U.S.A. Variety is the spice of life and if those brought up on traditional English games like Cribbage, Brag and Solo find in these pages some new games to play and enjoy, *Best American Card Games* will have served its purpose.

However the book is no mere dull encyclopaedia. Old games like Cinch, Schafkopf, Hasenpfeffer, Sixty-Six and Skat are excluded. They have been superseded by more modern games and are not much played today. Gambling games such as Faro, Pan and Ziginette are also omitted because they require special equipment and casino or 'house' arrangements. America is a vast country and for every major game there exists a large number of local and regional variants. Space is limited and so these too have been in the main ignored. What is left are fifteen games which represent the very best of the current American card playing scene.

It is never easy to learn a card game properly from a book, but at least in this volume, no knowledge is assumed on the part of the reader beyond the fact that a fifty-two card pack contains four suits of thirteen cards. The aim throughout has been clarity and completeness, even at the risk of sometimes labouring a point. Every game is fully illustrated by sample hands and deals to make the mechanics of play doubly clear. Also particular attention has been paid to those unexpected little problems and queries that inevitably crop up in the actual playing and which so many books tend to overlook.

There are extensive hints on play for each game. These may not mean much until the basic rules of the game itself have been fully mastered, but the enjoyment of a card game is immeasurably enhanced if it is played well. A close study of the advice they contain, combined with plenty of practice, will help the beginner become an accomplished player much more quickly than if he has to work everything out for himself.

American card games have a rich fascination all of their own and anyone who likes a hand of cards will certainly find something of interest here.

GIN RUMMY AND HOLLYWOOD GIN

GIN RUMMY

Gin Rummy is now the leading two-handed card game in the United States. Following very closely the rules of a Rummy variant much played around the turn of the century known as Gin Poker, it was taken up and popularised by an early Bridge expert from New York, Elwood T. Baker. Gin, as Baker called the game, spread rapidly during the Roaring Twenties. After a period of decline in the thirties, it became all the rage amongst the film colony of Hollywood at the end of the decade. As a result it achieved national prominence almost overnight. It was then that it acquired its present name of Gin Rummy.

The game is worthy of its popularity. Deceptively simple to learn and play, it demands a very high degree of skill to obtain the best results. The Lacework Kid, a fictional card 'pro' invented by short story writer Damon Runyon, could say lovingly of Gin Rummy that 'a moron is apt to play it better than Einstein', but in reality the average practitioner stands no chance against the expert player over an extended period.

HOW TO PLAY

As befits a national game, there is a large measure of uniformity everywhere about the basic rules of Gin Rummy. However the finer points have never been standardised, for efforts similar to those which succeeded with Contract Bridge did not produce an official codification of the laws.

The basic game is two-handed. The arrangements for games involving three players, called a 'Chouette', and for partnership games, two against two, are described later.

The standard pack of fifty-two cards is used. The sequence of the cards is natural: king, queen, jack, ten, nine, eight, seven, six, five, four, three, two, ace. So an ace follows a two but can never precede a king.

The idea of Gin Rummy is to collect sets of three or four cards of the same rank, or sequences of three or more cards of the same suit. For example, three or four queens, or three or four sevens constitute a set. Again the four, five and six of hearts, or the seven, eight, nine, ten and jack of spades make up a completed sequence. A sequence may extend to ten, the number of cards in each player's hand. Sets and sequences which satisfy the minimum requirement, that is contain at least three cards, count zero. Cards in hand that do not form part of a set or sequence are known as 'deadwood'. As deadwood, court cards (king, queen, jack) count 10, aces 1 and the other cards their numerical value.

The players cut for deal. Whoever cuts the higher card may deal himself or ask his opponent to do so. Thereafter the winner of one hand deals in the next. The winner of a completed game deals first if it is decided to play another game at the same session.

The dealer serves one card at a time face down, starting with his opponent, until both players have ten cards. The twenty-first card, called the 'upcard', is exposed on the table. The rest of the pack which forms the 'stock', is placed face down beside the upcard.

In the play, the two opponents try to make sets and/or sequences so as to reduce the count of deadwood in their hands to 10 points or less. Sets and sequences must be formed independently of one another. It is not permitted to use the same card as part of a set and a sequence. So combinations like king of hearts, king of clubs, king of diamonds, queen of diamonds, jack of diamonds are inadmissible. The king of diamonds must either be in a set of three or four kings, or in a sequence of diamonds, not both. On the other hand the cards can be arranged or rearranged in the hand in any way or at any time that a player chooses, for sets and sequences are not laid down on the table and exposed to the other player until the very end of the deal.

To begin play, the non-dealer has the option of taking the upcard into his hand or refusing it. If he does not take it, he must offer it to the dealer. If one or other of the players takes the upcard, he discards one card from his hand face up next to the stock. Should neither player want the upcard, the non-dealer draws the top card from the stock, puts it into his hand and then throws a card so as to cover the upcard. The dealer now has the choice of either picking up the card discarded by non-dealer, or the next card on the stock. After he has taken one of them into his hand, he also discards a card. Discards are placed neatly on top of one another in the waste pile and except for the last card, may not be looked at by the players during the hand.

The process by which each player either picks up the card most recently played by the other from the discards, or the next card from the stock, continues until one player elects to 'go down', or 'knock' as it is sometimes called.

A player may go down whenever the total deadwood in his hand numbers 10 or less. Suppose a player eventually holds a set of the kings of hearts, clubs and diamonds, and in sequence the queen, jack, ten and nine of clubs with three spare cards, the ace of clubs, the two of clubs and the two of spades. His deadwood count is $1 + 2 + 2 = 5$, and if he wishes he may go down. A player goes down after drawing in his turn. He announces his intention either by knocking the table before he discards or by making his final discard face down. He then exposes his ten cards on the table with his completed sets and sequences clearly separated, and apart from the unmatched deadwood cards.

Providing the player who has knocked has not gone down with a 'gin' hand, that is one containing no deadwood, his opponent may 'lay off' any cards from his own hand on the knocker's sets and sequences. He may not however lay off onto deadwood. Obviously in laying off, he does so without spoiling his own sets and sequences, but he is perfectly at liberty to rearrange his hand in such a way as to reduce it to the lowest possible count.

Say one player goes down with this hand for a count of 2:

♣Q ♣J ♣10   ♢9 ♢8 ♢7   ♣5 ♢5 ♡5   ♣2

Before play stopped, his opponent was holding his hand in the following way for its best possible score:

♢Q ♢J ♢10   ♣5 ♣4 ♣3   ♣4 ♣3 ♢3 ♣A

This gives a count of $4 + 3 + 3 + 1 = 11$ and if he puts down the cards according to this pattern, that will be his score on the deal. If however, having examined the knocker's exposed hand, he lays off his five of clubs on the set of fives and arranges the rest of his holding in this manner, he can improve his count:

♢Q ♢J ♢10   ♣3 ♣3 ♢3   ♣5 (laid off)   ♣4 ♣4 ♣A

Now his deadwood total is reduced to $4 + 4 + 1 = 9$, 2 lower than his best score whilst play was in progress. This might seem an insignificant amount but, as we shall see in a moment, even a few points may make a big difference to the final score in situations where the knocker's count can be matched or bettered by his opponent.

When both players have laid down the final versions of their hands, the two deadwood counts are compared. If the player who knocked can show a lower total of deadwood than his opponent, he scores the difference. So in the above example, the knocker has a count of 2 against his opponent's 9, for a net score on the deal of 7. The scores are recorded on paper. Every time a player wins a hand, the points he has made are added to the total of the previous points won, to make a new grand total.

It may happen however that after both hands have been laid down and counted, the opponent has an equal or lower deadwood score than the knocker. In this event the knocker is said to be 'undercut' and the opponent gets the difference between the two counts plus a bonus of 25.

Take for example these two hands:

Knocker: ♣ 7 ♣ 6 ♣ 5 ♣ 4 ♣ 3   ♢ 7 ♢ 6 ♢ 5 ♢ 4   ♠ 7

Opponent: ♠ K ♢ K ♣ K ♡ K   ♡ 8 ♠ 8 ♢ 8 ♣ 8   ♢ 3 ♠ A

The knocker has a count of 7, and even before any laying off he is already undercut, for his opponent has only 4 in deadwood. When the latter lays off his three of diamonds onto the knocker's diamond sequence, his count is reduced to just 1. So the opponent receives $7 - 1 = 6$, plus 25 for undercut, a score of 31 from the deal.

When the player who knocks has a hand made up entirely of completed sets and/or sequences, with no deadwood cards, he is said to 'go gin'. A typical gin hand could be:

♠8 ♣7 ♣6 ♣5   ♣5 ♣4 ♣3   ♡A ♣A ♢A

The bonus for gin is 25 points. This is added to the deadwood count in the opponents's hand. The opponent may not lay off any of his deadwood on a gin hand and a player who goes gin cannot be undercut. Even if by some chance the opponent also has a deadwood count of zero and through an oversight has failed to go down, the knocker alone scores the 25-point bonus. Against the above hand the other player might hold:

♣K ♣Q ♣J ♣10   ♡5 ♡4 ♡3 ♡2   ♠9 ♣4

Since the first player has a gin, the four and nine of spades may not be laid off on his sequence in spades and his score is $9 + 4 + 25 = 38$.

Occasionally a deal goes on and on without either player going down. Should play continue until there are only two cards left in the stock, neither of these cards may be drawn. The player who picks up the fiftieth card may knock, but if he merely discards without doing so, his discard may not be taken by the other player and the hand is a draw. This is known as a 'washout'. Neither player scores and after shuffling the cards, the original dealer serves out fresh hands.

A game is over when one or other of the players reaches a score of 100 or more from successive deals. First to 100 is awarded a bonus of 100. Each player also receives a bonus of 25 for every separate hand they have won. This is denoted by the line drawn under each score on the score sheet, called a 'line' or a 'box'. Bonuses are added to the cumulated scores from all the hands, and the lower grand total is deducted from the higher to arrive at a points winner.

If the losing player has not won a single hand during a completed game, this constitutes a 'blitz', also known as a 'shutout', a 'schneider' or a 'skunk'. In the event of an opponent being blitzed, the winner doubles his score as well as the game bonus of 100. The bonuses for boxes, however, are not usually doubled, unless the players agree to do so in advance.

Here is an example of a score sheet after a game between Jane and Bill:

	Jane	Bill	
B	17	46	A
F	34	62	C
		69	D
		75	E
		76	G
		101	H
		+100	
		+100	
		301	
		− 34	
		+267	

The actual hands might have gone like this:

Hand A: Bill goes gin and finding Jane with 21 in deadwood, scores 21 + 25 = 46.

Hand B: Jane knocks for 2. Bill's deadwood count is 19. Jane scores the difference and 17 is entered in her first box.

Hand C: Bill goes down for 10 and Jane has 26 in unmatched cards adding 16 more points to Bill's score, bringing it to 62.

Hand D: A further 7 points to Bill, when he goes down with 5 against Jane's 12 in deadwood.

Hand E: Bill scores another box and a total of 75 when he wins this hand by 6 points.

Hand F: Jane gets something back by knocking with 3 while Bill holds 20 in deadwood. 17 points are added to Jane's initial score to give a new total of 34.

Hand G: Bill goes down for 10 and Jane has only 11. Bill scores just 1 point but in addition gets another valuable box.

Hand H: Jane goes down with 6 but Bill undercuts her with his own deadwood count of 6. Bill scores a bonus of 25 which takes him up to 101 and game.

The final calculation is straightforward. Bill receives 100 points for the game. He has six boxes (A, C, D, E, G, H) worth 150 in bonuses, but Jane gets 50 for her two, so the difference of 100 is credited to Bill's side of the score sheet. 101 + 100 + 100 gives Bill a grand total 301, from which Jane's 34 points are deducted. Bill is the winner of the game by 267 points.

It is sometimes forgotten that with bonuses for boxes the player who first reaches 100 can actually lose at the finally reckoning. Take this set of scores for example:

Jane	Bill
6	54
17	102
32	+100
45	202
51	
68	
98	
+125	
223	
−202	
+21	

Bill scores 100 for game to give him a total of 202. However, Jane has 98 points from the successive deals. In addition she has won seven boxes to Bill's two, so she receives a net bonus from boxes of 125. Therefore Jane has amassed a grand total of 223 to Bill's 202 and wins by 21 points. Bill loses the completed game even though he was first to reach 100.

For the player who achieves the game score of 100 to eventually lose in this way is something of an anomaly. As we have already noted, there is no official set of rules for Gin Rummy and one important variant played by a significant minority of players is to adopt a different scale of bonuses to the usual one. The bonus for game remains 100 and a gin is still worth 25, but undercuts and boxes receive bonuses of only 20 points each. This reduces the chance of the first player to score 100 losing because of a big shortfall in boxes, as well as giving slightly greater credit for the difficult feat of going gin. So the '25 for gin, 20 for undercut, 20 for boxes' system has much to be said for it, even though it is not the most popular one.

THE PLAY OF A HAND

We will follow a full hand between Jane and Bill. Jane is the dealer. Therefore Bill has the first option of taking or refusing the upcard. The two players are dealt:

Jane: ◇Q ♣Q ♣J ♣10 ♡J ♡10 ♡8 ♣7 ♠6 ◇4

Bill: ♠Q ♠10 ♠8 ♡9 ◇9 ◇7 ♡6 ♠5 ♣A ♠A

Upcard: ◇8

Bill takes the upcard and discards the nine of hearts.
Jane takes the nine of hearts and discards queen of diamonds.
The hands are now:

Jane: ♣Q ♣J ♣10 ♡J ♡10 ♡9 ♡8 ♣7 ♠6 ◇4

Bill: ♠Q ♠10 ♠8 ◇9 ◇8 ◇7 ♡6 ♠5 ♣A ♠A

Bill could pick up the queen of diamonds but it would be a poor play. He will form a pair of queens but would be giving away information about his hand and he would have to discard a relatively low card that might be needed for keeping his deadwood to a minimum. Instead he draws a card from stock.

It turns out to be the king of diamonds. This does not help him at all and with Jane just having thrown the queen of diamonds, it seems a fairly safe discard. He puts down the king on the waste pile.

Jane has no use for this and draws the king of hearts. She decides to retain it in the hope of later picking up the queen to give her a six-card sequence in hearts. She discards the seven of clubs.

This will not improve Bill's hand and he takes nine of clubs from the stock. He does not really want the card but he has already seen Jane pick up one nine. She might want another. He keeps the nine of clubs and throws six of hearts.

Now the players hold:

Jane: ♣Q ♣J ♣10 ♡K ♡J ♡10 ♡9 ♡8 ♠6 ◇4

Bill: ♠Q ♠10 ♠8 ♣9 ◇9 ◇8 ◇7 ♠5 ♣A ♠A

Jane has both the eight of hearts and the six of spades and could well take the six of hearts, but any card at either end of her two completed sequences will enable her to knock. She draws from the stock, hoping to go down very quickly. She picks up the nine of spades. This is of no value to her. Bill has earlier thrown away a nine. It does not seem too dangerous for Jane to discard another. She throws the nine of spades away.

Jane has miscalculated. Bill does want her discard. He picks up the nine of spades. Surely, Bill thinks, he can now safely throw away the nine of clubs. He does so.

The hands are:

Jane: ♣Q ♣J ♣10 ♡K ♡J ♡10 ♡9 ♡8 ♠6 ◇4

Bill: ♠Q ♠10 ♠9 ♠8 ◇9 ◇8 ◇7 ♠5 ♣A ♠A

It is Bill who has miscalculated this time. Jane is not saving nines but she has a sequence of high clubs. She takes the discarded nine of clubs and throws away king of hearts face down to knock for a count of 10.
Her hand is:

♣Q ♣J ♣10 ♣9 ♡J ♡10 ♡9 ♡8 ♠6 ◇4

Bill is left with:

♠10 ♠9 ♠8 ◇9 ◇8 ◇7 ♠Q ♠5 ♣A ♠A

Bill's count of deadwood is $10 + 5 + 1 + 1 = 17$, none of which he can lay off on Jane's hand. Jane has scored 17 less 10 on the deal, to give her a box of 7.

In this relatively short hand, one of the many pitfalls for the unwary inherent in Gin Rummy is well illustrated. Any card has a potential double value, either as part of a set or of a sequence. Both Jane and Bill, watching the pattern of discarded nines, are lulled into a false sense of security. They both throw away nines to complete or extend sequences in the other's hand, ultimately at greater cost to Bill, who loses the deal.

HINTS ON PLAY

The Gin Rummy tyro is faced with many difficulties. Gin is not one of those games where the respective merits of one play compared with another can be calculated precisely. Rather, making the right decisions is very much a matter of flair. However there are a few simple techniques which any player can adopt that will certainly improve his game.

First of all, the hand should be arranged correctly. This is a point well worth making, for many Gin players commit the fundamental error of holding their cards in an illogical and unhelpful way. The hand should be put in a single sequence with the highest cards at one end and the lowest at the other. Within this arrangement, zero counts, pairs for potential sets and touching or near-touching cards which might eventually turn into sequences, should be grouped together as closely as possible. In this way a player can see at a glance what are his best and least chances.

During the play it is vital to try and remember all the discards. The waste pile yields information about what cards the opponent does not want and, by inference, those he does. Also by carefully memorising cards that have been thrown away, a player will be able to decide as the deal progresses which combinations in his own hand still offer the optimum prospects and which have been diminished in potential because some important card is buried among the discards.

Many players, even quite experienced ones, when they draw a card from the stock which they do not want simply throw it away without first putting it into their hand. This is foolish. It tells the opponent that the other hand has not been improved and may give him just the breathing space he needs. But he gains no clue about the progress of his rival if the latter slots unwanted stock cards into his hand and only makes a discard after a suitable pause. Moreover it definitely pays to examine every card very closely. The discipline of taking all cards into the hand may reveal possibilities that were not immediately apparent.

Some very complicated mathematics can be indulged in at Gin Rummy in an effort to assess exact odds and chances. In practice it is doubtful whether such calculations help greatly, for the game is in a constant state of flux and what the opponent will do is always an unknown factor. There is however one simple mathematical fact that should always be borne in mind. A set of three can only ever be improved by one card, while a sequence of three, except king, queen, jack or ace, two, three, can be improved by two. Further every sequence, unlike a set, can be extended beyond four cards. All other things being equal, this can give a clear-cut indication of what to save when choosing between several lines of play.

It is worth pointing out that most winning hands at Gin Rummy are made up of two, not three completed combinations when they are laid down on the table. So to avoid 'rag-picking' from the discards, some unmatched low cards such as aces, twos and threes, should be retained in order to reduce the deadwood count and enhance the prospects of going down for a low score.

All this is second nature to the expert player. On the other hand the expert looks at the game in a way that probably does not even occur to the beginner. For instance a really good player seldom picks up a card from the discard pile unless it completes a set or a sequence. Taking discards gives too many clues to the opponent. There are plenty of combinations which can be made up from the unseen stock cards alone, and the expert concentrates on these, whilst hoping that his rival will give the game away by drawing liberally from the waste pile. The novice has a single objective: to make the best of his own hand as quickly as he can. So he swallows up each and every card that seems to help, without a care for what cards he throws away. The skilful exponent of the game also aims to reduce his own count as quickly as possible, but he does so in such a way as to simultaneously thwart the other player. To this end he will rarely if ever throw away a card that he knows or suspects is wanted by his opponent. He forms an accurate picture of the other's hand and when his rival goes down first, he may well be able to undercut him by laying off.

Going down is obviously the most important phase of the game, but many beginners often get it wrong. At Gin Rummy it is usually correct to knock as soon as the opportunity occurs, unless there are strong grounds for fearing an undercut. To fight shy of going down with counts of 8, 9 or 10 is poor play, for there is little point in delaying merely to reduce such counts by just a few points. All this achieves is to give the opponent the chance to improve his hand, often quite dramatically. Anyone who has played a lot of Gin Rummy will be familiar with the player in danger of being blitzed who still fails to go down with a perfectly respectable count, preferring instead to hang on for a gin. There is only one thing to be done with such players. Offer them a game at the highest possible stakes. Perhaps one day they will learn the error of their ways!

GIN RUMMY FOR THREE

The most commonly played variant of Gin Rummy for three players is a 'Chouette', in which three participate but only two are in play against one another at any one time.

A single pack is used and a complete game is first to 100. The three players cut. Whoever cuts the highest card is 'in the box' for the duration of the game and has the choice of first deal against the player who cuts the second highest card. If the latter wins that deal against the box player, he plays the next hand and so on. However as soon as he loses a hand, the third player takes over and continues to play for as long as he goes on winning. In this way the two opponents of the player in the box alternate each time they lose a hand.

In the actual play the rules are the same as in the standard game, but the two in opposition to the box player may consult one another whilst a deal is in progress. The player who is sitting out therefore has a say in how his partner plays the hand, although this may cause dissension between players not blessed with an equable temperament!

One score is kept for the player in box position and one score for the other two. If the player in the box wins a game, he receives from each opponent his plus score. If he loses, he owes each of them the points value of his defeat. So for the player in the box the game is at double stakes.

The player in the box remains there until he is beaten in a 100-point game, whereupon the others cut to determine who shall take over from him. After two players have lost a completed game in the box, the third automatically goes there. When the third player completes his turn in the box by eventually losing a 100-point game, the cycle begins all over again with the box position reverting to the player who started the session there.

A session may last as long as is desired but it is customary not to terminate it until a full rota of all three players holding box position has been completed. If it is agreed to fix a limit to the number of games, the player in the box can be changed after each 100-point game regardless of who wins.

PARTNERSHIP GIN RUMMY

The four-handed version of Gin Rummy is for partners. Two separate games of two-handed Gin, using cards with different backs, are played simultaneously; but for each deal the partners enter their score as one.

The four players cut. The players who cut the two highest cards form one partnership against the other two. The partners sit opposite one another. The high-cutting players have choice of first deal in their respective games.

The rules are as in two-handed Gin Rummy except for the scoring. Each box is made up of a combined partnership score. Suppose Jane and Bill are playing as partners in opposition to Mary and Paul. Jane, playing the first hand against Mary, wins by 9 points. Bill loses by 12 points to Paul. 9 is deducted from 12 to give Mary and Paul a net score of 3 for the deal. If both hands are won by members of the same partnership, the two scores are added together to arrive at the team score on the deal.

In each succeeding hand partners play against alternate opponents. So in the second deal of our imaginary game Jane now swivels round at the table and plays Paul, whilst Bill plays Mary. On the next deal the games are again Jane against Mary, Bill against Paul, and so on.

A number of scoring schedules can be adopted. In one of the most common, game is 150 up. Gin, undercut and boxes are awarded bonuses of 25 each. Blitzes double both the game score and the game bonus of 100, but the bonuses for boxes are only doubled for a blitz if all the players consent before play begins.

HOLLYWOOD GIN

As we have already noted, it was the enthusiasm of the American movie world that turned Gin from just another card game into the principal two-handed game in the U.S.A. However, what particularly attracted the wealthy denizens of Beverley Hills was the invention of a system of scoring in which three Gin Rummy games are carried on simultaneously. Played for money, Hollywood Gin can be a very expensive game. What the American gambling community calls 'high-rollers' are in their element, but in the family circle there is no need for money to change hands at all. The Hollywood scoring system can be played simply as a way of adding interest and excitement to the basic game.

The essence of the Hollywood variant is that three columns, each representing a 100-point game, are scored for whilst play is going on. Only when all three games have been won and lost can a final reckoning be made to determine the overall winner.

The first time a player wins a deal his points are entered in the normal way in the initial column only. When he scores for a second time the additional points are again entered in the first column but they also go to form the opening box in the second column. The third time he wins a deal, the points now won are added to the scores already recorded in columns one and two, and they are also entered in the final column on the score sheet. Every time he subsequently gains a plus score from a hand, it is credited to each of the three columns.

When a player's score reaches 100 in a column, that column is closed and no further scores are added to it. The player receives his score, plus a bonus of 100 for the column, plus the usual bonus of 25 for every box he has won in excess of his opponent (if the first to 100 has scored less boxes than his opponent, the difference in the bonuses for boxes is added to the opponent's total as in the standard game). Then the points scored by the two players are compared to arrive at a net points winner for the column.

In the event of a blitz in a column, the winner's score, the game bonus *and* the bonuses for boxes are all doubled for that column. A blitz in one column does not preclude a player from scoring as normal in any subsequent column that has yet to be won.

Play continues until all three columns have been won by one player or the other, and this constitutes a completed game.

If one player has won all three columns, his net scores from each are aggregated to give his grand total of plus points. Should one player emerge as points winner in two of the three columns, the lower total score gained is deducted from the higher to arrive at a points winner from the three columns taken together as a single game.

This may seem a little complicated at first sight, so here is a full score sheet from a Hollywood Gin game between Jane and Bill:

Jane	Bill	Jane	Bill	Jane	Bill
18		21	41	5	18
39		26	59K	25	29
44		46		39	41
64		60		69	49
78		90		79	64
108A		100G		81Q	85
+100B		+100H			104M
+150C		+ 100I			+100N
358D		300J			+ 25V
× 2E		−59K			229P
716F		241L			−81Q
241L					148R
957S					
−148R					
+809T					

The boxes, bonuses and column totals are computed as follows to arrive at the final plus balance in favour of Jane:

Jane 18. 1st column only.
Jane 21. 18 + 21 = 39 1st column. 21 2nd column.
Jane 5. 39 + 5 = 44 1st column. 21 + 5 = 26 2nd column. 5 3rd column.
Jane 20. 44 + 20 = 64 1st column. 26 + 20 = 46 2nd column. 5 + 20 = 25 3rd column.
Jane 14. 64 + 14 = 78 1st column. 46 + 14 = 60 2nd column. 25 + 14 = 39 3rd column.
Jane 30. 78 + 30 = 108 1st column. 60 + 30 = 90 2nd column. 39 + 30 = 69 3rd column.
A 108   Jane's 1st column score.
B + 100 Bonus for winning 1st column.
C + 150 Bonus for six boxes.
D 358   Jane's 1st column total.
E × 2   For the column blitz.
F 716   Jane's final total in 1st column.
Bill 41. Bill's first score. 2nd column only.
Bill 18. 41 + 18 = 59 2nd column. 18 3rd column.
Jane 10. 90 + 10 = 100 2nd column. 69 + 10 = 79 3rd column.
G 100   Jane's 2nd column score.
H + 100 Bonus for winning 2nd column.
I + 100 Bonus for four boxes.
J 300   Jane's 2nd column total.
K − 59   Less Bill's 2nd column score.
L 241   Jane's final total in 2nd column.
Bill 11. 18 + 11 = 29 3rd column.
Bill 12. 29 + 12 = 41 3rd column.
Bill 8. 41 + 8 = 49 3rd column.
Bill 15. 49 + 15 = 64 3rd column.
Jane 2. 79 + 2 = 81 3rd column.
Bill 21. 64 + 21 = 85 3rd column.
Bill 19. 85 + 19 = 104 3rd column.
M 104   Bill's 3rd column score.
N + 100 Bonus for winning 3rd column.
V + 25   Bonus for one box.
P 229   Bill's 3rd column total.
Q − 81   Less Jane's 3rd column score.
R 148   Bill's final total in 3rd column.
F + L   716 + 241. Jane's totals from 1st and 2nd columns.
S 957   Jane's combined total from 1st and 2nd columns.
R − 148 Less Bill's total from 3rd column.
T + 809 Jane's winning total for completed game.

The Hollywood scoring system can also be used in Gin Rummy variants where more than two play. Obviously much longer games result when three columns, not one, are scored, and in a Chouette it will almost certainly be necessary to set a limit to the length of sessions by changing the player in the box after each three-column game is over. When there are partners, three columns of 150 points up constitute a game.

In Britain, Rummy is widely played as a nursery game. A seemingly easy contest spurned by serious card players, uncomplicated versions are a favourite amongst parents in search of distraction for bored children. The American variety is a very different kettle of fish and in the U.S.A. Gin Rummy is to two-handed card games what Bridge is to games for four players. Make no mistake, Gin is a very good game indeed and deserves equal popularity on this side of the 'pond'.

CONTINENTAL RUMMY

Few would disagree that Gin is the king of all Rummy games but it is really for just two players and cannot be played when a big social or family group wishes to join in. In Continental Rummy we have an exciting and enjoyable variant of the basic game that allows large numbers to participate. It has long been a favourite in the United States and although the advent of Canasta caused the loss of some of its adherents, it is still much played.

HOW TO PLAY

Any number from two to twelve can play Continental Rummy but four to eight make the best game. When up to five take part, two standard packs of fifty-two cards plus a joker for each are used. If six to eight play, three joker decks are needed, and in games of nine or more, four packs are shuffled together. It is immaterial whether the various decks have different or identical backs.

The cards from king to three run in their natural order, that is king, queen, jack, ten, nine, eight, seven, six, five, four, three. All twos (known as 'deuces'), like the jokers, are 'wild'. This means that their holder may use them in his hand to represent any other card in the pack. Aces can form part of a sequence headed ace, king, queen, or one beginning ace, two, three.

The players cut for deal. Ace ranks high and the player who cuts the highest card becomes the dealer. He serves out fifteen cards to each player including himself in batches of three, starting with the player to his left and going clockwise round the table. When everyone has fifteen cards the next card in the pack is exposed. This 'upcard' is the foundation of the discard pile and is placed alongside the remainder of the undealt pack, called the 'stock'. In subsequent hands the right to deal moves in rotation to the left.

Continental Rummy differs from most Rummy games in that only sequences in the same suit count, not sets of three or four cards of the same rank. There are also restrictions on the length and number of sequences that may be held. To go out, a player must lay down the whole of his hand as a single entity in one of these three combinations of sequences:

five 3-card sequences

three 4-card sequences and one 3-card sequence

one 5-card sequence, one 4-card sequence and two 3-card sequences

Bearing in mind that jokers and deuces are wild, here is an example of each of these three combinations:

♣Q 2 ♣10   ♣A ♣K ♣Q   ◇7 ◇6 ◇5   Joker ♡5 ♡4   ◇4 ◇3 Joker   (3-3-3-3-3)

◇A ◇K ◇Q ◇J   ♣J ♣10 ♣9 ♣8   2 2 ♠4 ♣3   ♠5 ♠4 ♣3   (4-4-4-3)

◇10 ◇9 Joker 2 ◇6   ♣9 ♣8 ♣7 ♣6   ♡6 2 ♡4   ♠6 ♣5 ♠4   (5-4-3-3)

During the play every player, beginning with the one immediately to the dealer's left, may take the face up card on the top of the discard pile, or the face down card at the top of the stock. After a player has drawn a card, he must straightaway throw one away from his hand to reduce it again to fifteen cards. The deal ends when someone is able to lay down, at his turn, one of the three legal hand patterns. Once one player has gone out in this way the other hands are dead, and losing players do not lay down their own sequences or lay off cards on the winning hand.

Sometimes the deal continues until the stock is exhausted and still no player has gone out. In this event the discard pile is turned face down without being shuffled to form a new stock for a second round of play.

A single deal constitutes a game. The player who wins the deal receives stakes from the others according to the following schedule:

For going out	1 unit
For each two contained in the sequences	1 unit
For each joker contained in the sequences	2 units
For a hand which contains no wild card	10 units
For a hand having fifteen cards of the same suit with or without the use of wild cards	10 units
For going out at the first turn	7 units
For going out at the first turn without drawing from the discard pile or stock	10 units

A hand may score for as many of the above as are appropriate.

SOME SAMPLE HANDS

Here are a few imaginary hands to demonstrate the legal combinations, the use of wild cards and how the scoring schedule is applied:

Hand A
♠K ♠Q ♠J ♠10 ◇6 ◇5 ◇4 ◇3 ♣6 ♣5 ♣4 ♣3 ♣8 ♣7 ♣6

For this hand, laid down after a number of draws from the stock and discards, its holder scores 1 for going out and 10 because it contains no joker or deuce. Each of the losing players therefore pays 11 units.

Hand B
♣K ♣Q ♣J ◇10 ◇9 ◇8 2 ♡9 ♡8 ♣6 Joker ♣4 ♣5 ♣4 ♣3

The player who eventually goes out with this hand receives from his opponents 1 for going out, 2 for the joker it contains and 1 for the deuce, a total of 4 units.

Hand C
◇A ◇K ◇Q ◇J ◇10 ◇9 ◇9 ◇8 ◇7 ◇7 ◇6 ◇5 ◇5 ◇4 ◇3

After several rounds of play, one player is lucky enough to go out with this hand for a total score of 21; 1 for going out, 10 because it contains no wild cards and 10 because all the sequences are in diamonds.

Hand D
♡K ♡Q ♡J ♡10 ♡9 ♡J 2 ♡9 2 ♡9 2 ♡7 ♡6 ♡5 Joker

This 5-4-3-3 hand might be from a game involving seven players where three decks are in use. One player eventually wins the deal with it and scores 1 for going out, 3 for three deuces, 2 for a joker, and 10 because the sequences are all made up of hearts. The other players thus pay 16 units each. If its holder had the good fortune to be dealt such a hand, he would go out immediately without drawing. He would then receive 10 rather than 1 for going out, and the hand would be worth 25 units in all.

Hand E
♡Q ♡J 2 ♡9 Joker ◇10 2 ◇8 ♠6 ♠5 Joker ♠3 Joker ♣4 2

Imagine a player is dealt the above cards except that they contain some unmatched card, say the king of clubs instead of the ten of diamonds. He cannot go down at once but after taking a card from the stock at his first turn he picks up the ten he needs to complete the sequence in diamonds. He throws away the unmatched king of clubs and scores 7 for going out at the first turn. In addition he scores 6 for three jokers and 3 for three deuces. 16 units are owed him by each of his rivals.

HINTS ON PLAY

Although definitely an improvement on simple Rummy, Continental Rummy is still basically a game of luck rather than skill. However there are one or two points the beginner should note.

Even with the jokers and deuces as wild cards, it is not always easy to collect a winning hand quickly, for when more than two play, a player does not have access to every discard. In a game where the turn to draw moves in rotation to the left round the table, he can only take the cards thrown away by the player who immediately precedes him at his right. The difficulty of making up a completed hand is further increased by the limitations set upon the pattern of sequences that are acceptable for going out. It pays therefore to take any card which helps the hand, even though it may come from the discard pile. In Gin Rummy this is generally regarded as poor play because it yields too much information about what a player is saving. In Continental Rummy also, taking exposed discards provides clues on which a right-hand opponent may later act. It must be remembered however, that once the player to the right has rejected a card for his own hand, he is more or less committed to discarding other cards that are next or near to it in rank and suit. He will throw away such cards in the interests of his own hand even though he suspects they may be wanted by the opponent whose turn comes immediately after his.

Suppose for example, that one player discards the six of hearts because it is of no value to his hand and it is taken from the discard pile by the next player. If he subsequently draws the five of hearts, this too is unlikely to be of any use to him. Without another safe discard and unless he is prepared to spoil his own hand, he must throw away the five despite knowing that the player after him probably wants it to go with the six picked up earlier.

So in Continental Rummy there are few opportunities for defensive play. The best strategy is to watch carefully which cards have been thrown away by other players and thus become inaccessible, and after assessing a hand in relation to these, to pick up any card that improves it. Discards should be from definitely unhelpful cards, without worrying too much that they could assist the next player. The player who looks solely to his own hand nearly always does best at the game in the long run.

Continental Rummy rightly remains a popular game among all sorts of Americans. The use of more than one pack of cards and the introduction of wild cards, combined with a coherent system of scoring and bonuses, turns the basic Rummy game for lots of players from a somewhat insipid affair into an exciting battle for supremacy.

FIVE HUNDRED

Most card games evolve naturally over a long period of time and finally achieve a form that is generally accepted. Five Hundred on the other hand was deliberately invented in the early nineteen hundreds by the United States Playing Card Company as a counter-attraction to the then prevailing craze for Auction Bridge. Auction gave way to Contract, but even today Five Hundred remains an important part of the American scene.

There was never any serious attempt to promote the game in this country and for that reason it has largely been overlooked in Britain. This is a pity, for apart from being a game of considerable skill, one of its chief merits lies in the fact that it incorporates many of the elements of Bridge, yet can be played by three or even two players.

HOW TO PLAY

Five Hundred is derived from Whist and is a trick-taking game. Depending on the strength of the cards they have been dealt, players can bid to make six or more tricks from a ten-card hand, in a trump suit of their own choosing. The value of bids is determined by a scale based on the rank of the suits taken in conjunction with the number of tricks contracted for. The player who makes the highest bid in the auction then tries to win enough tricks to fulfill his contract, whilst his opponents play together in an attempt to stop him.

Any number from two to five may play, but the game is ideal for three players and the three-handed version is therefore described first.

When three play, the twos to the sixes are omitted from a full pack. The addition of one joker makes a thirty-three card deck.

The rank of the cards differs for trumps and the three side suits. In trumps the order is: joker (highest), jack ('right bower'), jack of the other suit of the same colour ('left bower'), ace, king, queen, ten, nine, eight, seven (lowest). In the other suits the normal Whist order applies: ace, king, queen, jack (provided it is not left bower), ten, nine, eight, seven.

In bidding the suits rank: hearts (highest), diamonds, clubs, spades (lowest). Players may opt to play without trumps and a no-trump bid outranks any suit call for a similar number of tricks.

The three players cut for deal. Ace ranks high and the player who cuts the highest card deals. In subsequent hands the deal passes in rotation to the left. The dealer begins by serving out three cards at a time to each player, starting with the one immediately at his left. He then lays out three cards face down on the table. These form the 'widow'. The deal is completed by each player receiving a batch of four more cards and then a final three, so that everyone has ten cards. Since some or all of the widow may eventually form part of the highest bidder's hand, this means that the whole of the thirty-three card pack is in play during the game.

In the bidding phase of Five Hundred, each player has one chance to bid or pass. The player to the dealer's left calls first and the dealer himself last. Bids are made on an estimate of a hand's trick-taking potential, bearing in mind that whoever wins the auction can nominate trumps or choose to play without them, and has the option of using the widow cards. Once a bid has been made, any subsequent bid by another player must be of a higher points value according to the following table:

	6 tricks	7 tricks	8 tricks	9 tricks	10 tricks
As trumps:					
Spades	40	140	240	340	440
Clubs	60	160	260	360	460
Diamonds	80	180	280	380	480
Hearts	100	200	300	400	500
At no-trumps:	120	220	320	420	520

POINTS VALUE

Suppose the player at the dealer's left makes a bid of 'six clubs'. This has a points value of 60. Second player in the auction must make a call of a higher value if he wishes to become contractor. If he feels he cannot do so, he passes. But say he thinks he has a good hand provided he can nominate diamonds as trumps; he could bid 'six diamonds', worth 80, and so make the best call so far. If in fact he has well above average cards, with plenty of diamonds, and is reasonably confident of taking more than the minimum six tricks, he may decide to bid 'seven diamonds' for a value of 180. The dealer who is last to call has an indifferent hand and passes without hesitation. The player who said 'six clubs' cannot bid again and 'seven diamonds' thus becomes the contract. The second player is now committed to making at least seven tricks with diamonds as trumps, against the combined efforts of his two opponents.

There is one other bid that could have been made which is not shown in the above table. This is 'nullo'. Ranking higher than a call of 'eight spades' but lower than 'eight clubs' and worth 250 points, the nullo bid is an undertaking to take no tricks at all. The opponents play together against its caller to try to force him to win at least one trick. Obviously a player only goes nullo with a very weak hand. As with any bid which becomes the contract, the player who calls it has the right to use the widow in making up his final hand. At nullo there are no trumps.

Should all the players pass in their turn, the cards are thrown in and the next player who has the right to deal shuffles the cards and serves out fresh hands for a new round of bidding.

Once a contract has been decided upon, the next stage is to deal with the widow. Without showing them to his opponents, the contractor picks up the three cards from the table and puts them with his original ten cards. From the thirteen he now holds he chooses the ten he thinks most likely to help him make his bid. The three unwanted cards are discarded face down on the table. The other players may not look at them and they may not be referred to by the contractor for the rest of the hand.

The contractor leads first and may put down any card he chooses. Subject to the different rank of the cards in trumps where the joker, right bower and left bower head that suit, Whist rules apply. So each of the players plays one card to a trick. They must follow suit to the card led if able. If they cannot do so, they may trump or discard from a side suit; at no-trumps they can only throw away from some other suit. No player is obliged to try to win a trick if he does not wish to do so. A trick is taken by the highest card played of the suit led, or by the highest trump when one or more of the players cannot follow suit and plays a trump. The winner of a trick leads to the next.

As tricks are played, the players keep their own winners before them and separate on the table; for although two combine against the contractor in an attempt to defeat his bid, each opponent will achieve an individual score on the hand depending on how many tricks he himself takes.

Most trick-taking games are played without a joker, so in Five Hundred special rules are needed to determine its correct play. When there are trumps, the joker is the highest trump. It belongs to the trump suit alone and has no 'wild card' status as in other games. It may also be used like any other trump to win a trick when a suit is led in which its holder has no cards.

At no-trumps, or nullo, the joker is again the highest card in the pack and automatically wins any trick to which it is played. However the joker may not be used when its holder can follow to the suit led. When a player leads the joker in a no-trump or nullo contract, he must specify the suit the others must play to if they can. Again the joker wins the trick. On the other hand he cannot nominate a suit which he has already renounced in play. For example, if he has indicated that he is out of spades by discarding a card of some other suit on an earlier round of spades, he cannot subsequently ask for spades to be played to the lead of the joker.

When the ten tricks have been played out, individual scores are counted for the deal.

If the contractor makes at least as many tricks as he bid, he scores the points value of his bid, but he receives nothing for any extra tricks. So if he bids 'seven diamonds' and wins nine tricks, he scores only 180. If however he wins all ten tricks, he receives 250 or the value of his bid, whichever is the higher.

Should the contractor fail to make the required number of tricks, the value of his bid is deducted from his total score. So minus scores from one or a series of hands are possible in Five Hundred. It is usual to draw a ring around a minus total and the player is said to be 'in the hole'.

Whether a bid is made or defeated, each opponent scores 10 points for every trick he himself wins during the deal. For example if the contractor bids and makes 'seven diamonds' but loses three tricks, two to one player and one to the other, the former scores 20 and the latter 10 points.

The only exception to this is that in a defeated nullo bid, the opponents both receive the same score. No matter at what point the contractor wins a trick, the hand is played out to the end and each opponent gets 10 points for every trick taken by the contractor. As in other calls, the contractor loses only the value of his bid, that is 250, irrespective of how many tricks he is forced to win.

Scores for individual hands are added to, or subtracted from, each player's total until 500 is reached by one player who thereby wins the game.

Should the contractor and one or more other players get to 500 on the same deal, the contractor wins against an opponent or opponents. This is so regardless of the precise point in play at which the 500 scores are achieved. An opponent might score 500 first by winning tricks, but if the contractor subsequently makes his bid and reaches 500, he and not the opponent is the winner. This rule is sometimes the source of misunderstanding and dispute. Yet it is perfectly fair and logical. Tactical necessity may require the contractor to win tricks later rather than sooner, and he must be given the chance to justify his call.

Between opponents to the contractor however, the first to reach 500 by tricks wins. In this case the hand is not played out to the end unless the contractor could also score 500 by making his bid. If any player claims game by virtue of winning tricks before a deal is completed, he must expose the remainder of his cards to demonstrate that he has played legally and is not guilty of a revoke.

THE PLAY OF A HAND

Mary, Jane and Bill sit down to a game. Mary cuts the highest card and deals, first to Jane, then to Bill and finally to herself in batches of three, four and three cards.

Jane is first to bid. She picks up her hand and this is what she sees:

Joker ♡K 7 ◇A K Q 10 ♣— ♠K Q 10

This is not a bad hand at all and is definitely worth a bid. It contains the joker and with diamonds as the trump suit Jane must make at least three trump tricks and perhaps four if the remaining trumps are favourably distributed between the other two hands. She should also make one of the two high spades provided trumps are drawn quickly and no one can take advantage of a shortage in spades to trump in on a round of that suit. With luck the king of hearts might win as well. Six tricks is by no means impossible, especially if the widow comes up with some extra help. Jane bids 'six diamonds'.

Bill's hand is as follows:

♡10   ◇9 8 7   ♣10 8 7   ♠J 8 7

These are a poor lot. A nullo bid might succeed but the ten of hearts looks very exposed. Bill decides not to gamble on help from the widow and passes.

Mary however has dealt herself a good hand:

♡A Q J 9 8   ◇J   ♣A K J   ♠9

Holding both right bower and left bower in a heart bid, she should only lose to the joker in trumps, so she has five near-certain winners. The ace and king of clubs should also win tricks barring accidents.

Mary bids 'seven hearts', worth 200 points if she succeeds and becomes contractor. She now picks up the widow which is:

♣Q 9   ♠A

It is Mary's lucky day! She keeps the ace of spades and queen of clubs, and discards the nine of clubs plus her jack of clubs and nine of spades.

The hands are now:

Jane: Joker ♡K 7   ◇A K Q 10   ♣—   ♠K Q 10

Bill: ♡10   ◇9 8 7   ♣10 8 7   ♠J 8 7

Mary: ♡J◇J♡A Q 9 8   ♣A K Q   ♠A

Mary, as contractor, leads her highest trump, the jack of hearts which loses to Jane's joker. Jane has no clubs and would dearly like to get her partner Bill to lead so that he can return a club she can trump. She must hope Bill has the ace of spades but even if he does, will he overtake her king with it and play back a club? Hopefully Jane puts down the king of spades but Bill can only play the seven and Jane knows her fate. Mary wins the trick with the ace of spades, draws Jane's last two trumps with the jack of diamonds and the ace of hearts, and plays off the rest of her trumps and the three top clubs for a total of nine tricks.

Mary scores 200 for her seven hearts bid but nothing for the two extra tricks she has taken. Jane receives 10 for her one trick. Bill fails to score.

HINTS ON PLAY

A good Five Hundred player needs to be a precise but imaginative bidder. The game is highly competitive and generally speaking it pays to bid a hand to the limit of its strength. This is certainly true of minimum hands where normal bidding requirements should be stretched in order to call six or seven of a suit. With strong hands on the other hand it is often better to err on the side of caution.

In suit bids there are ten trumps, so ideally five are needed to cope with most adverse distributions in the hands of the opponents. When estimating the trick-taking potential of a trump suit, it is reasonable to count, in addition to high-card winners, one trick for each card held above four. So joker, right bower, queen, eight, seven will produce two certain tricks plus one probable winner for the fifth card, with the remaining high trumps in the opponents' hands able to capture two tricks. Some players, in stretching a bid on a problematical hand, count a trick for each trump in excess of three. This is a highly speculative procedure and can prove costly. It is based on the assumption that the enemy trumps are placed most favourably to the bidder's advantage. In practice this is not always the case.

With long, strong trumps it is also sound to count for length in a good side suit. One trick for every card over four is a fair expectation, even if some of the top cards are missing. However a trump suit which guarantees control throughout the hand is vital, for if his opponents can weaken the contractor's trumps by forcing him to trump losers early on, he may eventually run short of the trumps necessary to dominate the end play. If this happens, even the high cards in a second suit are vulnerable and he will have no chance of 'bringing in' its long cards.

Aces and king-queens are obviously worth one trick in side suits, but king and a small card is only a possible trick and not certain to win.

Most no-trump bids succeed by contractor developing a long suit at the expense of high cards and any long suit held by the opponents. Therefore at least a five-card suit is desirable for a call of no-trumps. Again it is safer to count cards over four rather than three as probable 'long card' winners. As well as having a long suit, for a no-trump bid to succeed the player should hold a stop in each of the other suits. If the opponents can establish a long suit of their own quickly, they may gain the lead and win tricks with small cards on which contractor must discard winners. In this connection the joker can be very useful as a stopper in an otherwise exposed suit. On the other hand holdings like king and another, or queen and two others are very vulnerable in no-trump contracts.

The unseen widow is an important part of bidding estimates. Whilst it is unreasonable to expect to find a specific card in the widow, a player making a bid is entitled to expect some help from the three spare cards. On calls of six or seven the widow will often, but not always provide at least one extra trick. With really strong hands however, it is dangerous to look for any additional assistance at all. Expectations of the widow should also be modified whenever a strong bid, or indeed a bid of any kind, has already been made by some other player.

When using the widow cards, contractor should as far as possible strengthen long suits and discard unwanted low cards from short suits, provided they are not needed for the protection of a high card like a king or a queen without the ace.

In the play of the hand there are two basic strategies for contractor. In suit calls he should lead trumps in order to pull two of his opponents' to one of his own, and he should go on drawing trumps as long as he is certain of retaining control of them. However it would be foolish to continue pulling them to the point where he has none at all or where his own trumps are inferior to those of his rivals, thereby leaving himself vulnerable in any unprotected side suit. At no-trumps contractor should lead his longest suit, even if he is lacking the top cards in it, and keep playing it at every opportunity in the hope of establishing its long cards. He should use high cards in side suits only as stops and re-entries. Similarly opponents will play any long suit they have, whenever they can, with the object of eventually making long, small cards in it.

At suit bids the opponents do best if they avoid opening up new suits. If contractor is trumping a suit, they should play it each time they get the lead. This gives nothing away and may pay a handsome dividend. Contractor can only make his small trumps once and if he can be brought to a position where he has no trumps left, the opponents may be able to run a suit in which they have both strength and length. The exception is when one of the opponents has better trumps that contractor himself. In this case they should lead them at him. Being weak in trumps, contractor will now want to trump into suits in which he is void. By playing trumps themselves his rivals reduce his chances of doing this and if he ultimately runs out of trumps, again they may be able to run a suit where they are strong and he is weak.

In general play the opponents should bear in mind that contractor is most exposed from his right-hand opponent who leads through him, rather than from his left-hand adversary who leads up to him. In other words his intermediate high cards are most vulnerable from the right.

TWO-HANDED FIVE HUNDRED

The best version of two-handed Five Hundred is played with a twenty-four card deck. All cards below the nines are removed from a full pack and the joker is dispensed with. Each player receives the usual ten cards, but this time the widow consists of four cards. The rules of bidding, play and scoring are as in the three-handed variant, except that a player who reaches a minus score of 500 loses the game just as one who achieves a plus of 500 wins it.

Since there are now only seven trumps headed by the right bower and the left bower, the bidding standards for this version of the game are much less stringent. A four-card trump suit is far more acceptable, and counting long cards in excess of three is standard practice. Bids can be stretched to the limit with a much greater prospect of success, especially when a call has been made to which the second player to bid has little defence. High bids of a speculative nature, dependent on a lot of assistance from a four-card widow, may succeed when they would almost certainly fail in variants of the game involving more than one opponent in which only three extra cards are available. In the two-handed game the composition of an opponent's hand can be estimated far more accurately, with the contents of the widow as the only problematical factor. Possible adverse distributions between two enemy hands do not enter into calculations at all.

Another two-handed variant is to use the thirty-three card deck as in the game for three players, but to deal a completely dead hand face down on the table. Play is with two hands of ten cards and a three-card widow. With ten cards out of play, bidding is little more than a guesswork and much of the skill is removed from the game.

FOUR-HANDED FIVE HUNDRED

Four-handed Five Hundred is a partnership game. Partnerships can be by agreement or cutting. Partners sit opposite one another at the table.

A forty-three card deck is used, made up of the aces to the fives in all suits, the two red fours and a joker. From this deck each player receives ten cards and there is a widow of three cards. The players as before have only one bid each. When one player becomes highest bidder he and his partner must together make the tricks required by the bid. The other partnership plays in tandem to try to prevent them doing so. Scores from bids by the contracting side, or from tricks won by the opposing team, go towards a partnership total. The first side to reach 500 wins and as in the two-handed game, a partnership which records a minus score of 500 loses. All other rules are as in the standard game, except for the case of nullo. When nullo becomes the contract in a partnership game the contractor's partner throws in his hand face down and contractor plays alone against the opposite side. He and his partner receive the usual 250 should he succeed in not taking a trick. If he does win a trick, his side loses 250 points and the opponents add 10 points to their total for each trick taken by him.

The four-handed game of Five Hundred is difficult to play well, for the first player to bid has no idea what his partner holds and with each player having only a single call, there is no exchange of informative bids as occurs in Bridge.

FIVE-HANDED FIVE HUNDRED

The standard fifty-two card pack is used, plus the joker, to give each player ten cards and a three card widow. When a round of bidding has been completed the highest bidder names any player he wishes to be his temporary partner for that deal. If he has contracted for eight or more tricks, he nominates any two partners. The remaining players play together to try to defeat the bid. A player who becomes contractor with a nullo bid plays alone against the other four. Five individual scores are kept and the game is 500 up. Temporary partnership scores are added to each individual total at the completion of a hand.

All the versions of Five Hundred have much to recommend them. Less scientific than Contract Bridge, the game is nonetheless a very fair test of card skill, and has the advantage over Bridge of not being confined to four players.

OH HELL

Oh Hell is sometimes more politely called Oh Pshaw or Blackout. The game's origins are obscure but it began to be played in America in the 1930's and has been popular ever since. At first sight Oh Hell may seem to involve an unacceptable level of guesswork and luck. However a closer examination of the finer points of the game reveals plenty of opportunities for skilful bidding and play.

HOW TO PLAY

The regular pack of fifty-two cards is used and the cards rank as at Whist: that is ace (high), king, queen, jack, ten, nine, eight, seven, six, five, four, three, two (low).

Oh Hell follows very closely the basic rules of Whist whilst incorporating a simple form of contractual bidding. The number of cards dealt to each player increases as the game proceeds and the idea is that players try to estimate exactly how many tricks they will make on a given deal, from none at all up to the maximum available on the round. Only those players who make precisely the number of tricks they have bid, not more or less, score.

The game may be played by any number from three to seven players. The total number of deals which constitute a complete game varies according to how many participate as follows:

three-handed : fifteen deals; one to fifteen cards in a deal

four-handed : thirteen deals; one to thirteen cards in a deal

five-handed : ten deals; one to ten cards in a deal

six-handed : eight deals; one to eight cards in a deal

seven-handed : seven deals; one to seven cards in a deal

So on the first round each player receives one card, on the second two cards, on the third three cards, and so on right up to the maximum fixed by the number of players.

At the start of the game players cut for the deal in the usual way. Ace ranks high and the player who cuts the highest card becomes the first dealer. Thereafter the right to deal moves round the table to the left.

The dealer serves one card at a time to each of the players in rotation. He begins with the player at his left and gives each the correct number of cards due on the deal. The card at the top of the pack after the deal is completed is turned face up. Its suit determines trumps for the round being played. The very last deal of the game however, is always played without a trump suit, so no turn-up card is exposed on the final round.

Players now take it in turns to bid, beginning with the player at the dealer's left and moving round the table in the same direction as the deal. There is only one chance to bid. Taking into account the strength of their hands, particularly in relation to what suit is trumps, players bid the number of tricks they believe they can make from zero up to the maximum possible. So on the first deal only two bids are possible, zero or one. In the final deal of say a three-handed game, a player may bid for any number of tricks from none up to fifteen.

It is customary to appoint a scorekeeper for the duration of the game. The score sheet is divided into two columns per player. In the left-hand column the scorekeeper records the individual bids of all the players for the round being played. During the bidding any player may ask the scorekeeper what bids have gone before, and at its completion it is the duty of the scorekeeper to announce whether the deal is overbid, even or underbid. In other words he says whether the total of the players' bids adds up to more than, the same as, or less than the number of tricks available on the deal.

Since the object of the game is to make only the number of tricks bid, the players are trying to lose as well as win tricks, in the hope of finishing the deal with the correct total. The player at the left of the dealer leads any card to the first trick. One card from each player constitutes a trick. Players must follow suit to the card led if able. If they cannot follow, they may trump or discard from a third suit; at no-trumps they merely discard from another suit. There is no obligation to try to win a trick if a player does not wish to do so. A trick is won by the highest card played of the suit led, or by the highest trump played if one or more players cannot follow suit and decide to play a trump. The winner of a trick leads to the next. Tricks won are kept in separate piles in front of the players who have captured them.

When all the tricks have been played each player assesses his score for the deal. If he made exactly the number of tricks he bid, he scores that number plus 10. This total is entered in the second column on the score sheet opposite his bid for the deal. If however he has won more or less tricks than he bid, he is said to be 'bust' and he scores nothing for the round.

A player who made a bid of zero and who succeeded in not winning a trick, scores the number of tricks available on the deal plus 5. So if there were five tricks in the deal, a successful zero bid would gain a score of 5 + 5 = 10. By this system of scoring, zero bids attract progressively higher scores as the game proceeds, since it is held to become more difficult to make no tricks at all as the number of cards in a deal increases.

After the round at no-trumps has been played and the number of deals called for in the game is thereby completed, the scorekeeper adds up the grand total of points scored by each player. The player with the highest total is the winner.

A GAME OF OH HELL

On the next page is the full score sheet of a game between Jane, Bill, Mary and Paul over the thirteen deals in the four-handed version of Oh Hell. On the right of the score sheet proper is a table of the actual number of tricks taken by each of the players on the various deals.

The fourth deal for example contains four tricks. Jane bid for two tricks. In fact she made only one and was therefore bust for no score on the round. Bill contracted for one trick but did not make any. He too scored nothing. Mary bid zero but was forced to win a trick. She did not score either. Alone of the four, only Paul made something from the deal. He bid and won two tricks and received credit for the two plus a bonus of 10, a score of 12.

On deal number six Jane bid and made one trick for a score of 11. Bill got 12 for his successful bid of two. Paul bid zero and did not win a trick, so he scored 6 for the number of tricks in the deal, plus 5 for his correct call, making 11 in all. Mary who bid two but actually won three tricks, was bust and failed to score.

After the thirteenth and last hand Mary with a grand total of 81 emerged as the overall winner.

HINTS ON PLAY

Oh Hell is well named, for such are the frustrations inherent in the game that players may well find themselves moved to utter some violent expletive, at least under their breath. Except when the sum total of the bids is equal to the number of tricks in a deal, each player has a different objective. So to make the exact number of tricks according to what has been bid is frequently a much harder task than it might at first appear.

The game is not made any easier by the fact that bidding is very far from being an exact science. It should be remembered that tricks are on the whole easier to lose than to win. For this reason it is usually safer to underbid rather than overbid a hand. Many experienced players make a practice of estimating the number of tricks they are likely to take and

Number of tricks in the deal	JANE Bid	JANE Score	BILL Bid	BILL Score	MARY Bid	MARY Score	PAUL Bid	PAUL Score
1	0	6	0	6	1	11	1	–
2	1	–	1	–	1	–	0	7
3	0	8	1	11	1	11	1	11
4	2	–	1	–	0	–	2	12
5	2	–	1	11	2	–	1	–
6	1	11	2	12	2	–	0	11
7	2	–	0	12	3	–	5	–
8	3	13	1	–	0	13	4	–
9	2	–	2	12	4	–	0	–
10	4	14	3	–	4	–	1	–
11	2	–	5	–	6	16	2	–
12	3	–	3	–	3	13	3	13
13	4	–	2	12	7	17	2	–
		52		76		81		54

JANE	BILL	MARY	PAUL
0	0	1	0
0	2	0	0
0	1	1	1
1	0	1	2
3	1	1	0
1	2	3	0
1	0	0	6
3	0	0	5
1	2	5	1
4	4	2	0
3	2	6	0
4	2	3	3
3	2	7	1

deliberately underbidding that number by one. This will not always succeed but it has much to recommend it as a basic bidding strategy.

The dealer always has a slight advantage over his rivals. If he finds himself in doubt as to what to bid, he is often in a position to make the round even. As a result he may get help from the other players. Should everyone achieve their respective bids, he, like them, will record a plus score which is better than no score at all. However, with a clear-cut hand the dealer should bid what he estimates to be its exact value, and if there is some room for error, make the total of the bids uneven. His opponents may then cut each other's throats, and allow him an element of choice which will enable him to make the tricks he has bid.

In evaluating the trick-taking potential of a hand, high and low cards are relatively easy to assess but intermediate cards like sevens, eights and nines present a considerable problem, especially on the earlier rounds where so many unknown cards remain undealt in the pack. In fact in the early stages of the game not even high cards are safe. When the players have only a small number of cards the likelihood of someone being void in a side suit means that the danger of having even apparently certain winners trumped is ever present. This can upset the nicest of calculations.

There are no easy answers. A vast number of distributions of the cards are possible. The correct line of play is subject to the various and often contradictory aims of the other players who in their own interests will sometimes assist it and sometimes thwart it. These factors give Oh Hell its unique fascination, and make flexibility and the ability to manoeuvre successfuly the hallmarks of a good player.

Oh Hell will never be one of the giants among card games but its very unpredictability brings a high level of interest and the chance to respond to fluid situations by the exercise of card sense and technique.

HEARTS, BLACK LADY AND OMNIBUS HEARTS

Hearts games are played according to the fundamental principles of Whist, but the object of play is the reverse of most trick-taking games. There are no rewards for making tricks, only penalties for any cards of the hearts suit that players are forced to win. Since poor hands in the conventional sense are now at a premium, Hearts is the perfect antidote to those Whist and Bridge players who always seem to be complaining about the bad cards they receive. However, the game is very much one of skill. So those who also do badly at this game will need to change their excuse and curse the gods of fate for sending them too many high cards!

HOW TO PLAY

Hearts may be played by any number from three to six players. There are no partnerships, so whatever the number who participate, each plays for himself.

The standard fifty-two card pack is used when four people play, but certain low cards are removed if there are more or less than four players. So in a three-handed game the two of clubs is put on one side in order to give each player seventeen cards instead of the usual thirteen. If five take part, only ten cards are dealt to each player, and the two of clubs and two of diamonds are removed from the full deck. With six players each begins with just eight cards, the twos of clubs, diamonds and spades and the three of clubs having been discarded.

In all four suits the cards rank in Whist order: ace (high), king, queen, jack, ten, nine, eight, seven, six, five, four, three, two (low). Every hand is played without trumps.

The player who cuts the highest ranking card deals. Thereafter the deal moves round the table to the left. The dealer gives one card at a time in rotation to each player, starting with whoever is at his immediate left, until the whole pack has been distributed.

The player at the dealer's left leads. Each player in rotation to the left plays one card to a trick. Players are not obliged to try to win a trick, but they must follow to the suit led. If they are unable to follow suit, they may play any card they wish. A trick is won by the highest card it contains of the suit led. The winner of one trick leads to the next.

Since hearts are penalty cards, each player tries to avoid winning tricks which contain cards of that suit.

A number of scoring systems are used for Hearts. Three of the most sensible are:

i) The score is kept with pen and paper. 1 point is added to each player's cumulative score for every heart they win on a deal. When after a series of hands one player reaches 50 (or sometimes 100) points, the deal in which this occurs is completed, the final penalties are added to each player's running total and the game ceases. The player with the lowest overall cumulative score is the winner. If the game is played for stakes, each of the losing players pays to the winner the difference between their respective scores. Here is an example from a 100-point game between Jane, Bill, Mary and Paul.

Jane	Bill	Mary	Paul
61	94	103	71

Jane is the winner. She receives from Mary $103 - 61 = 42$ units, from Bill $94 - 61 = 33$ units and $71 - 61 = 10$ units from Paul.

ii) Sometimes the game is played with a pool. In a family game every player receives so many chips, say 50 each. If the game is for money, chips represent cash and a player takes as many chips as he wishes to play for.

For every heart a player takes on a deal, he puts one chip into the pool. The player who has taken the fewest hearts wins the pot. If two or more players tie for the lowest hearts score, the pool is divided equally between them and any odd chips that remain are carried forward into the pool for the next deal.

iii) Another popular pool game is 'jackpots'. When a deal is completed, each player contributes one chip to the pot for every heart he has won in his tricks. If only one player is 'clear', that is has taken no hearts at all, he scoops the pool. If two or more players are clear on the deal, they split the pool between them and any odd chips go into the following pot. However should all the players be 'painted', that is they have all been forced to win hearts, or if all thirteen hearts have been taken by a single player, then the pool is said to be a 'jack'. It remains intact on the table for the next deal. The first player or players to be clear on some subsequent hand collect the whole of the accumulated stakes from the normal losing contributions to the pot, plus any jack or jacks.

THE PLAY OF A HAND

Here is a full deal between Jane, Bill and Mary which should make the mechanics of the game itself absolutely clear, whatever scoring system is adopted.

Bill

♡ Q J 5

♠ K 8 5 4 2

♢ 10 7 6 5 2

♣ K 9 5 3

Jane (dealer)

♡ 10 8 7 2

♠ J 10 9 7

♢ A K 9 8 4

♣ Q J 8 7

Mary

♡ A K 9 6 4 3

♠ A Q 6 3

♢ Q J 3

♣ A 10 6 4

Jane	Bill	Mary
	♣ K (opening lead)	
		♣ A
♣ Q		
		(Mary's trick)
		♡ 3
♡ 2		
	♡ Q	
	(Bill's trick)	
	♣ 9	
		♣ 10
♣ J		
(Jane's trick)		
♠ J		
	♠ K	
		♠ A
		(Mary's trick)
		♡ 4
♡ 10		
	♡ 5	
(Jane's trick)		
♡ 7		
	♡ J	
		♡ 9
	(Bill's trick)	

Jane	Bill	Mary
	♠ 2	
		♠ Q
♠ 10		
		(Mary's trick)
		♣ 4
♣ 8		
	♣ 5	
(Jane's trick)		
◇ 9		
	◇ 10	
		◇ Q
		(Mary's trick)
		◇ J
◇ 8		
	◇ 7	
		(Mary's trick)
		♣ 6
♣ 7		
	♣ 3	
(Jane's trick)		
♡ 8		
	♠ 8	
		♡ 6
(Jane's trick)		

Jane	Bill	Mary
◇ 4		
	◇ 2	
		◇ 3
(Jane's trick)		
♠ 7		
	♠ 5	
		♠ 6
(Jane's trick)		
♠ 9		
	♠ 4	
		♠ 3
(Jane's trick)		
◇ K		
	◇ 6	
		♡ A
(Jane's trick)		
◇ A		
	◇ 5	
		♡ K
(Jane's trick)		

So at the final count Mary has won five tricks but no hearts. Bill made only two tricks but they each contain three hearts, making a total of six against him. Jane has been forced to take ten tricks which include seven hearts. Jane has done worst on the hand, but given the cards she was dealt, this outcome was predictable. She had nothing but high and middle cards, with just a single low one, the four of diamonds, in the side suits. Only her reasonable hearts holding saved her from total disaster. From the middle of the deal onwards her lack of low cards meant she was left in the lead and was unable to lose it, so Mary could discard her remaining hearts on the tricks Jane was forced to win.

HINTS ON PLAY

The secret of good play at Hearts is to count the cards whilst the hand is in progress. This is not as difficult as it may seem. Rather than trying to keep track of each individual card as it goes down on the table, the trick is to make a mental note of how many rounds of a suit have been played, bearing in mind any discards by players who were unable to follow. It is then a relatively simple task to work out what number of cards still remain in the suit. It is also important to remember as play proceeds which card is the lowest outstanding in each suit. Armed with these two pieces of knowledge, a player is in a much stronger position than if he simply plays to the suit led and looks no further than his own hand. Does he play high or low to an opponent's lead? If he plays high and wins the trick, is he likely to get a heart discard later in the round because no other cards are left in the suit? If he wishes to lose the lead, can he be sure of doing so by playing a certain card in the absolute knowledge that someone else must play a higher one? How many hearts are still to be played and if he goes on leading hearts, will he eventually be forced to win a trick in them? The answer to questions of this kind vitally affect playing technique at every stage of the hand. Carefully counting the cards in the recommended manner will nearly always supply the necessary information on which to act.

It pays to assess the hand before play begins in order to decide what tactics are likely to produce the best result. A good first lead is from a short side suit which should subsequently be played at every opportunity. The idea is to get rid of all the cards in the suit so as to have the chance of later discarding hearts and other dangerous cards when an opponent leads it.

Any high card in any suit is potentially dangerous but on the first couple of rounds of a side suit it is fairly safe to play out aces, kings and queens. However the risk of heart discards develops very quickly. Generally speaking, the more players there are, the greater the chance of a discard on an early round of a suit.

On the other hand it is not always best to immediately throw a heart at the first opportunity to discard. It may be wiser to strengthen a vulnerable side suit by getting rid of a risky card in it. Very high cards guarded by a lot of low ones are usually safe to keep, but high to middle cards from jack down are full of danger if unsupported. Such holdings should be led from early in the game and discarded from whenever possible.

The play of the heart suit needs special care. A player holding several very low hearts should play them whenever the lead is gained, provided of course there are enough of them to protect any high hearts which might be forced to win tricks later on. By leading small hearts one player compels the others to win the penalty tricks and reduces the chances of them discarding hearts on him. However, with a single top heart and no very great length in the suit, it is often best to sacrifice by using the high card to win an early round of hearts. If the high heart is retained and it takes a trick towards the end of the deal, its holder may be left with the lead, and unable to lose it, receive a stack of discarded hearts. In playing from side suits it is also a good idea to keep back a very small card, a two or a three, to be used to get off lead in the final stages of the hand.

Provided it is done legally, without actually discussing tactics before or during play, it is perfectly legitimate for players to combine against an opponent who is well ahead in the scoring, although in a friendly game this may cause friction. In pool games also, players may help one another to paint a rival who has yet to win a heart and so seems likely to take the pot.

BLACK LADY

Black Lady is an extension of Hearts with the additional feature that the queen of spades is a minus card which counts 13 against the player who is unfortunate enough to win it in a trick. Cards of the heart suit continue to have a penalty value of 1 point each. A single card therefore assumes paramount importance in this game and the hearts are relegated to a secondary role. A number of variants, usually called Black Maria, are played in Britain, but the American version includes the concept of 'shooting the moon' which is peculiar to the game as it is played in the United States.

HOW TO PLAY

Apart from the status of the queen of spades, the basic rules in regard to the make-up of the deck according to how many play, the deal and the play of the hand are exactly the same as in Hearts. There is however one extra rule in Black Lady which is of the utmost importance. This is the 'pass'. After the cards have been dealt but before a card is led to the first trick, each player must pass on three cards to his left-hand opponent. The procedure is for every player to put the three cards selected for passing face down on the table. Only when all the cards are on the table may the players pick up the three new cards they have received from their right-hand opponent. So by means of the pass there exists an opportunity for all to improve their original holdings by getting rid of dangerous cards, although the situation may be worsened again to a greater or lesser extent by the fresh cards that are received.

Black Lady is never played with a pool, scoring always being by the cumulative method. After every deal the penalty points collected by each player are added to their respective running totals for the game. If however one player wins all thirteen hearts and the queen of spades in the same deal, he is said to 'shoot the moon'. Instead of being penalised 26 points, he gains that number for accomplishing the difficult feat of a 'take-all'. 26 points are deducted from not added to his cumulative score.

The game ends when one or more players reach 100 after the completion of a deal. The player with the lowest overall score wins. The losing players pay the winner the difference between their respective losing and winning scores.

HINTS ON PLAY

All the advice contained in the hints on play section for Hearts applies equally well to Black Lady. In Black Lady however two further points need to be considered: the pass, and the play of the spade suit.

The pass usually has a great influence on the ultimate destination of the queen of spades. The two top spades, the ace and the king, are obviously dangerous cards to hold because they may eventually be forced to capture the Black Lady. Unless they are guarded by at the very least three other spades below the queen, either or both of them should certainly be passed on. Some players pass them automatically, however well protected they seem and regardless of what other risky cards they have. There will be times when this tactic pays off.

The queen of spades is safer in a player's hand than in someone else's unless he does not have adequate control over it. Thus if he is dealt the Black Lady with only a couple of spades or less to guard her, he should pass her. Otherwise she may well win a trick after only a few rounds of spades have been played. A player handing on the queen who also has the ace or king must obviously pass them as well. With the Black Lady and a minimum of three other lower spades it is usually correct to keep her and try to drop her under the ace or king, or take the first chance during the play to discard her.

High hearts are risky cards and provided the player has no problems in spades they should be passed on. Even middle hearts are poor cards to have if there are no low ones in support, and make good passes. However it should be no surprise if, having handed on dangerous hearts, more of the same are received from right-hand opponent. For this reason low hearts (twos, threes, fours, etc.) should always be retained.

Dealt a very good hand with no natural discards from spades or hearts, a useful pass is from a short suit to give a player the chance of an early discard from any undesirable cards he might receive from the right. On the other hand spades below the queen should never be given away. If the Black Lady is passed on, its recipient will need all the length in spades he can muster.

During the play, except for a player who holds a vulnerable ace or king of spades, those who do not have the Black Lady should lead spades to try to drive her out before she can be discarded on one of them. The holder of the queen of spades on the other hand must never lead spades as a general strategy of play. The only time he is justified in making a spade lead is when the spade suit is almost cleared and he knows for certain that the ace or king must drop over his queen.

The 'take-all' is a fascinating feature of the American game but a player should only try to shoot the moon when his hand appears almost certain to achieve it, for the penalty for a near failure is very high. Should some player seem to be going for a take-all with real prospects of success, one opponent must be prepared to try and step in and win a heart trick he need not otherwise have taken in order to thwart the 26-point bonus.

OMNIBUS HEARTS

Omnibus Hearts has now become the most popular variant of the Hearts group of games. It is in fact an extension of Black Lady.

HOW TO PLAY

As before, there is a three-card pass before play actually begins, each heart won has a penalty value of 1 and the queen of spades carries a penalty of 13, but in this game the ten of diamonds attracts a bonus of plus 10 for the player who takes it in a trick.

The fact that the ten of diamonds is now a bonus card does not alter its status in the play. It can only be played as a diamond and continues to rank below the jack and above the nine of that suit.

Shooting the moon remains an important feature of the game but now a player must capture all thirteen hearts, the queen of spades *and* the ten of diamonds to get a 36-point bonus for the take-all.

So in the scoring, plus 10 for the ten of diamonds or plus 36 for take-all are deducted from the cumulative minus scores from hearts and the queen of spades. The game terminates when one player reaches a grand total from successive deals of minus 100. The player with the lowest minus total is the winner.

A GAME OF OMNIBUS HEARTS

The juggling of plus and minus scores called for in Omnibus Hearts may be a little confusing, so here is a full score sheet from a game between Jane, Bill and Mary.

Jane	Bill	Mary
+8 (+10−2=+8)	−13 (−13=−13)	−11 (−11=−11)
−10 (−13−5=−18)	−8 (+10−5=+5)	−14 (−3=−3)
−16 (−6=−6)	−11 (+10−13=−3)	−21 (−7=−7)
−19 (+10−13=−3)	−16 (−5=−5)	−29 (−8=−8)
−22 (+10−13=−3)	−20 (−4=−4)	−38 (−9=−9)
−27 (−5=−5)	−11 (+10−1=+9)	−58 (−13−7=−20)
−18 (+10−1=+9)	−25 (−13−1=−14)	−69 (−11=−11)
−27 (−9=−9)	−17 (+10−2=+8)	−84 (−13−2=−15)
+9 (+10−13−13= take-all=+36)	−17 (———)	−84 (———)
−3 (−12=−12)	−17 (———)	−88 (+10−13−1=−4)
−10 (−7=−7)	−36 (−13−6=−19)	−78 (+10=+10)
−6 (+10−6=+4)	−39 (−3=−3)	−95 (−13−4=−17)
−17 (−11=−11)	−30 (+10−1=+9)	−109 (−13−1=−14)

The figures in brackets show how each player scored on a deal. +10 indicates the winning of the ten of diamonds, −13 the queen of spades and any other minus figure the number of hearts taken. After the = sign is the total, plus or minus, from the deal. The cumulative score from all the hands is at the left-hand side of each column.

In the final deal Mary won the queen of spades and a heart to lose 14 points and take her past the minus 100 point. Jane with an overall score of minus 17 is the winner.

HINTS ON PLAY

Although clubs are now the only neutral suit, the fundamental principles of sound play at regular Hearts and Black Lady apply to the Omnibus version. The top spades and all the hearts except the very lowest are liabilities. Diamonds on the other hand are a double-edged weapon. High diamonds are needed to capture the ten for a 10-point bonus, but they may be forced to win tricks on which the Black Lady or hearts are discarded by other players.

One of the best strategies is to expect to be painted from time to time with the queen of spades and some hearts, and to aim to capture the ten of diamonds whenever possible as a way of reducing minus scores. For this reason the ace of diamonds and the court cards of the suit should not be passed, but the ten of diamonds itself is seldom won by the player who holds it after the pass. A player who is dealt the ten should hand it on to his left-hand opponent and try to recapture it in a trick with a high diamond or by a forced discard at the end of the deal.

The play at Omnibus Hearts usually divides itself into two distinct phases. In the first the Black Lady is the biggest danger and players try to get rid of their risky cards and to avoid winning any trick on which she might be discarded. With the queen of spades out of the way, the objective is then to win the ten of diamonds. As explained above, it is often best to play for the ten even if this involves collecting a few hearts in the process. The chances are that a net plus will result.

The take-all in Omnibus Hearts is very, very difficult to bring off. Success depends on holding an exceptional hand with most of the important high cards. Low hearts which cannot be passed on or which are received from the right make a take-all nearly impossible. However aces, though desirable, are not absolutely necessary. Even the ace of hearts in certain fairly rare cases is not essential. As in Black Lady, the penalty for a near-miss is severe, especially when the ten of diamonds happens to fall to some other player. On the other hand when someone does successfully shoot the moon, it is very costly for all his opponents. One player should be prepared to win a round of hearts unnecessarily to prevent it. However it is dangerous to overdo this tactic. If a sacrifice involves a player winning more than a single round of hearts, he will gain very little from it because of the large number of hearts points conceded to all the other players, and if as a consequence, he is forced to collect nearly all the hearts, it will constitute a personal disaster for him.

Whether preference is for Hearts or Black Lady, both are games in which the object is to lose rather than win the most important tricks, and therefore make an interesting diversion from other varieties of Whist. They deserve a wider audience in this country, and those who already play the English variant of Black Maria will find Omnibus Hearts a fascinating extension of the game.

KLABBERJASS

Klabberjass is an international game. The name itself, pronounced 'klahbur-yahss', is German for the jack of clubs, the highest trump in most old Central European card games. The modern version seems to have developed from a Hungarian game, *Kalabrias* which is for three or four players. The two-handed variant described below was brought to the New World by German immigrants and nowadays Klabberjass is often abbreviated to Clob, Clobber, Clabber, Clubby, Klob or Klab. It is very like the French national game of *Belotte*, although there are significant differences in points of detail. It is curious that Klabberjass is virtually unknown in any form in this country. Alone among English games, Piquet has some similar features and may be a distant relative.

HOW TO PLAY

Klabberjass is played with a deck of thirty-two cards, the twos to the sixes inclusive having been removed from the regular fifty-two card pack.

The rank of the cards differs between trumps and the side suits. In trumps the order is jack (high), nine, ace, ten, king, queen, eight, seven (low). The trump jack is called the 'jass' (pronounced 'yahss'), the nine of trumps is known as the 'menel' (pronounced 'muhnell', with the accent on the second syllable) and the seven of trumps is the 'dix' (pronounced 'deece'). In the other three suits the cards rank ace (high), ten, king, queen, jack, nine, eight, seven (low).

On each deal there are several objectives. First, each of the two players attempts to get his best suit made trumps. The player whose bid determines the trump suit becomes the 'maker'. The maker must achieve a better final score than his opponent. If he fails to do so, he is heavily penalised. During the play both players score for holding certain combinations of cards and try to win tricks that contain high ranking cards which have a points value.

The players cut for deal. Whoever cuts the lower card, with ace ranking high, becomes the dealer for the first hand. Thereafter the deal alternates throughout the game.

The dealer gives a batch of three cards to his opponent and three to himself, then a further three to his opponent and three more to himself, so that each of them begins with six cards. The next card from the pack is exposed face up on the table. The suit of this 'turn-up' influences the bidding as the possible trumps.

The non-dealer makes the first bid. There are three bids he can make. Firstly he may 'take', that is accept the suit of the turn-up card as trumps, thereby becoming the maker, and the bidding is at an end. Alternatively he may 'schmeiss' (pronounced 'schmice'). The schmeiss bid is an offer to throw in the hand or to play with the turn-up suit as trumps, the choice being made by his opponent. If the opponent accepts the schmeiss there is a fresh deal, but if he refuses it, the bidding is over, the turn-up card determines trumps and the non-dealer is the maker. Finally non-dealer may pass. In this event the right to bid passes to the dealer.

The dealer has the same three bidding options: take, schmeiss or pass. If he does not take or make a schmeiss proposal, he passes and there is a second round of bidding.

Now the non-dealer has a choice of another three bids. He may name any of the other three suits as trumps, becoming the maker in the suit he specifies. Or he may schmeiss, by which he offers to abandon the deal or to play as maker in some other suit without however naming it at this stage. Again the dealer may accept the schmeiss and the cards are thrown in, or he may refuse and ask the schmeisser to state the suit he wants to make trumps. Thirdly the non-dealer can pass again, in which case the dealer names another suit as trumps or passes in his turn. Theoretically the schmeiss is also available to the dealer on this round of bidding, but since his opponent will almost certainly ask for the deal to be abandoned, it is a pointless bid and is never made. Should the dealer not wish to become maker, his pass means that the hand is finished and the non-dealer takes over as dealer for the next hand.

Once trumps have been decided upon, the dealer gives a further batch of three cards first to his opponent and then to himself. Finally he turns up the bottom card of the pack and places it face up on the table alongside the original turn-up. This extra card is dead as far as the play of the hand is concerned, but serves to provide additional information to the players which may influence their tactics.

Should one player hold the dix, he may now exchange it for the original turn-up provided that the suit of that card has been made trumps. He thereby obtains a higher trump than the seven. The non-dealer must make this exchange before he leads to the first trick, but the dealer may strictly speaking take it after the non-dealer has played a card. However in some circles the exercise of this privilege is regarded as bad form, and the dealer too exchanges the dix before his opponent makes the opening lead.

The players then compare sequences. A sequence consists of a minimum of three consecutive cards in the same suit and here the cards run in their most natural order, that is ace, king, queen, jack, ten, nine, eight, seven. A sequence of three cards counts 20; one of four or more 50.

Only one of the players may score for sequence, so a dialogue is necessary to establish who has the higher. If the non-dealer has no sequence at all, he says 'No sequence' or 'May I lead?' and the dealer then calls the points value of any sequence he wishes to score for. If he has no sequence himself, he says so and non-dealer leads to the first trick.

If the non-dealer does hold one or more sequences, he announces the value of the best of them–'Twenty' if his best sequence is one of three cards, or 'Fifty' if it contains four or more cards. If the dealer has no sequence, or one of inferior value, he says 'Good' and non-dealer scores. If the dealer can beat his opponent's sequence, he says 'Not good' and receives credit for his better holding. Should he hold a sequence of equal value to that called by the non-dealer, he asks 'How high?' The non-dealer then announces the top card of his sequence. At this stage he has no need to name the suit, just the denomination of the card. The dealer replies by saying whether this is good or not good and the player with the sequence headed by the higher ranking card scores. If both players claim a sequence of equal points value headed by cards of identical rank, a trump sequence beats one in a side suit. If both players hold equal non-trump sequences, traditionally the non-dealer's wins. However, many exponents of the modern game think this unfair and in the event of absolute equality, the points for sequence are not scored. This is a matter to be agreed upon between the players before the game begins.

The order of comparison of sequences is always the same: points value first, top card of the sequence second, and trumps last. However, there is no difference in points value between sequences of four, or five or more cards–all are worth 50. Comparisons between these are therefore by highest card, and trumps or non-trumps.

As soon as one player acknowledges that his opponent's sequence is good, the latter exposes it and scores its points value. He also scores the value of any other inferior sequences he happens to hold which are as yet unannounced. The losing player scores nothing.

The key to the sequence dialogue is the proper use of the responses 'Good', 'Not good' and 'How high?' which ensures that each player provides just the minimum of information necessary to establish who has the higher sequence. Thus cards need only be exposed by the player who claims the points.

Here is an example. Spades are trumps and Mary is dealer against Bill. The hands are:

Mary: ♠A 7 ◇K ♣Q ♡Q J 10 9 8

Bill: ♣Q J 10 9 ◇10 ♣10 9 8 ♡A

The dialogue would then run thus:

> **Bill**: 'Fifty.' (for his spade sequence)
> **Mary**: 'How high?' (she holds a sequence in hearts also worth 50)
>
> **Bill**: 'Queen high.'
> **Mary**: 'Queen.'
>
> **Bill**: 'Trumps.'
> **Mary**: 'Good.'

So Bill scores 50 for his spades sequence and another 20 for his three-card sequence in clubs. After exposing both sequences, he receives credit for a total of 70 points. Mary, though she has five hearts in sequence to the queen, loses to Bill's four-card trump sequence which is also headed by the queen, and does not score.

It is one of the finer points of the game that a player is not compelled to announce any sequence he holds for which he does not wish to claim. Suppose one player says 'Fifty' for a sequence of four cards. The other also holds a four-card sequence but knows from the make-up of his hand that it must be inferior. In this case he need not ask 'How high?' but simply says 'Good', thereby conceding the points. In this way he does not have to reveal information that may be tactically useful to his opponent in the subsequent play of the hand. It is even within the rules for a player to fail to reveal a winning sequence if he thinks that he may gain more in the play by not disclosing it. For example should he believe that secrecy will later yield 40 points in the play, he may decide to give up 20 points for a low winning sequence. It must be said however that such tactics are only in the realms of expert play.

When the points for sequence have been settled, irrespective of who has become the maker, the non-dealer leads a card. Bearing in mind the unusual and different rank of the cards in trumps and side suits, the hand is played out in nine tricks, each player putting down one card to a trick. Second player to a trick must follow suit if he is able, and when he cannot follow the suit led he must play a trump if he has one and so take the trick. If a side suit is led, the second player need not win the trick if he does not choose to, always provided that he can follow suit. But when a trump is led he must win the trick if he can. A trick is won by the higher trump played or should it contain no trump, by the higher card of the suit led. The winner of one trick leads to the next.

Whilst play is in progress, there is only one possible scoring combination. This is 'bella'. When one player holds both the king and queen of trumps in his hand, he scores 20 for them by announcing 'Bella' when he lays down the second of the two, regardless of who wins the tricks to which the cards are played. If a player forgets to call 'Bella' at the appropriate time, he may not score for it later. On the other hand he may deliberately refrain from announcing it should the state of the play make such an expedient seem advisable. This would be so when as maker he seems in real danger of conceding all his points to his opponent rather than scoring for them himself (see below for 'bete').

The main object of play is to win tricks containing valuable cards, which are counted up when the hand is over. Tricks as such do not score, except that a player receives 10 points for winning the very last trick, called 'stich' and pronounced 'stish'.

The values of high cards won in tricks are as follows:

Jass	20
Menel	14
Each ace	11
Each ten	10
Each king	4
Each queen	3
Each jack (except jass)	2

When the deal is at an end, each player counts up the points he has won in tricks and adds any scores for sequence, bella and stich. The totals achieved by the two players are then compared. If the trump maker has the higher total, each player is credited with what he himself has scored. But if the maker has a *lower* total than his opponent, he is 'bete' (pronounced 'bate'), and his opponent scores the sum of the two totals. If the counts are exactly equal, the maker is 'half bete'. The maker then scores nothing at all while his opponent is credited with the points he himself has scored.

A game is decided over a series of successive deals. The first player to reach a total of 500 points at the end of a deal wins. If both players reach 500 on the same deal, the one who has achieved the higher of the two scores after the deal has been completed is the winner.

THE PLAY OF A HAND

Here is a full deal played by Mary and Bill. It is the first hand of a new game, so neither has scored. Bill cuts the lower card and becomes dealer.

The hands are:

Bill (dealer): ♠10 ♢— ♣A J 8 ♡Q 8

Mary: ♠9 ♢A K ♣10 Q ♡7

Turn-up: ♢Q

Mary, as non-dealer, bids first. She holds ace and king in the turn-up suit and a guarded ten of clubs outside it. However, she lacks the jass or menel in diamonds and is not strong enough to take. She could schmeiss and risk playing as maker in diamonds should Bill refuse to abandon the deal, but this would serve no great purpose and is almost as dangerous as an outright take. Bill might have a good hand and could even hold jass or menel himself. In that case Mary would be in deep trouble. She quite rightly decides to pass.

Now it is Bill's turn to bid. He cannot stand diamonds and wants to make clubs trumps. He has a good chance of coming out on top in that suit but he must first wait and see what Mary does on the second round of bidding. He too passes.

Mary looks at her hand again. Perhaps if she had the jack of spades instead of the nine, she could schmeiss, thereby denying Bill the opportunity to call his suit. She has an ace and a ten in the other suits and provided her hand was improved by the three extra cards to come, she might succeed as maker in spades. It is a difficult decision, but the fact that she is missing the jass finally tips the balance in favour of a pass.

Bill has good clubs with the jass, and an outside ten, for which the additional cards will possibly provide a guard. He names clubs as trumps and is the maker. Bill deals out the fresh cards and turns up the king of hearts from the bottom of the pack.

The hands become:

Bill (dealer): ♣J A 8 (trumps) ♡Q 8 ♠10 ♢10 J 9

Mary: ♣10 K Q ♡7 ♠9 7 ♢A K 8

Turn-up: ♢Q Bottom card: ♡K

Mary, as non-dealer, says 'May I lead?', indicating that she has no sequence. Bill however holds jack, ten, nine of diamonds. He claims 20 and shows Mary the three cards. Mary now plays to the first trick.

Bill	Mary
	♡7
♡Q	
(Bill's trick)	
♣J	
	♣Q
(Bill's trick)	
♡8	
	♣10
	(Mary's trick)

Bill	Mary
	♠ 9
♠ 10	
(Bill's trick)	
◇ 9	
	◇ K
	(Mary's trick)
	♠ 7
♣ 8	
(Bill's trick)	
◇ J	
	◇ A
	(Mary's trick)
	◇ 8
◇ 10	
(Bill's trick)	
♣ A	
	♣ K ('Bella')
(Bill's trick)	

Bill has won the last trick and counts 10 for stich. In addition to his 20 for sequence, he has captured in the tricks jass (20), one ace (11), two tens (20), one king (4) and two queens (6) for a score of 91 on the deal. Mary has taken three tricks which contain an ace, a ten, a king and a jack for 27. With 20 for bella, her total is 47.

Bill has won the hand easily and his decision to become maker in clubs has been fully justified. He scores 91 towards game, whilst 47 go on Mary's side of the score sheet.

HINTS ON PLAY

The minor catastrophe of going bete is an ever present danger in Klabberjass. That is why good players are content to 'bury' so many hands without a bid. On an average deal there is a total of somewhere between 100 and 120 points available. Since about 20 points is a fair expectation from the three cards dealt after trumps have been made, a player needs to hold

35–40 in the first six cards to give the balance of points which justifies a take. Jass, menel, any other high trumps and outside aces and tens should be counted at their face value. Whilst it is wrong to hope for a specific card from the extra three, they will usually supply a guard for a bare ten, so these too should be assessed at their full worth of 10 points.

However, the dealer must be prepared to lower the minimum requirement for a take after his opponent has passed. By 'shading' he denies non-dealer the choice of trumps he would get from another chance to bid. On the other hand with a defensive holding, that is one having good overall strength with several jacks and nines, players in both positions should try to let the opponent become maker, in the hope of catching him out.

For the maker, jass and menel are far more important than trump length. Any hand lacking at least the menel, if not the jass, runs the risk of going bete, and many four-card trump holdings without them suffer this fate, much to the surprise of inexperienced players. By contrast, even a singleton jass supported by good cards in the side suits succeeds more often than not.

The schmeiss bid is a very subtle weapon for the skilful player. Both non-dealer and dealer can use it on the first round of bidding with a hand not quite good enough for a safe take but better at the suit of the turn-up card than any other. This is something of a risk but for the dealer one which is often worth taking, for he knows his rival is not keen on the turned up suit as trumps because he has passed. Like a shaded bid, the schmeiss effectively stops the non-dealer from later naming a good suit of his own as trumps. By contrast the non-dealer should be very wary of schmeissing immediately, in case he is forced to become maker and finds himself 'clobbered' for a huge bete score by a powerhouse hand held by the dealer. The risk is so great that some players never schmeiss on the first round as non-dealer; but precisely because the bid is so infrequent, non-dealer can sometimes use it to frighten his opponent out of a superior hand. Even then, the occasional bluff of this kind requires good tolerance for trumps and some outside strength, for the dealer may suspect a bluff and refuse to abandon the deal though he has only a moderate hand.

Too many psychological schmeisses which lack the playing strength to back them up may well prove very expensive in the long run, particularly against good players. But the non-dealer can and should use the schmeiss on the second round provided he has a fair hand with a goodish suit to name as trumps. By schmeissing after the dealer has passed, it is the non-dealer this time who prevents his adversary from calling his own best suit. Now the dealer must either throw in his hand or play with a trump suit in which he might have little or nothing. Since he does not know for certain what will be trumps, the dealer is always tempted to quit.

Several strategies are possible in the play, depending on the make and shape of a given hand. Generally speaking, if maker has four or more trumps, he should draw those of his opponent at once, thereby reducing the latter's chances of trumping high cards in side suits. Without length in trumps however, it is dangerous to pull them prematurely. Maker must try to keep trump superiority throughout the deal, holding one trump back if possible to make sure of stich. Left with no trumps for the closing tricks, he may lose the lead and have to throw high cards on side suit winners in non-maker's hand.

In the normal course of events non-maker should let trumps be played to him. After maker's top trumps have been led out, he could well win a trump trick or two which contain ranking cards. The best lead for non-maker is from a four-card suit or a sequence of three cards which he goes on playing at every opportunity. With not much in the suit, maker may be forced to use up valuable trumps quickly, and non-maker might establish a low card during the end play if his opponent's trumps are limited. Employing these tactics, he can at the same time retain any short suit ace to capture a ten if maker has to play one. This is important for, after trumps, aces and tens are the really vital cards in the play. Though easier said than done in a two-handed game of only nine tricks, both players should as far as possible avoid or at least defer leading out aces and tens. Ideally an ace should be used to capture the opponent's ten when he has been forced to lead it.

One final point is that beginners tend to ignore stich. Yet the outcome of many deals depends on it, for the difference between winning and losing the last trick represents a 20-point swing in the score. Good players design their tactics in such a way as to give themselves the very best chance of taking what is often the decisive trick.

Klabberjass is a big money game in many parts of the United States. It has that blend of skill and luck, combined with the opportunity to bluff, which appeals to seasoned card gamblers. But even without the spice of a substantial stake, Klabberjass is one of the best of all games for two players.

PINOCHLE

Pinochle, pronounced 'peenockle', is the American version of Bezique. It is hardly known in Britain, but though largely superseded in recent years by Gin Rummy as the principal two-handed game in America, it remains among the leading half dozen card games there. The game described below is the standard one, from which many local variants have been derived. Pinochle is not particularly difficult to learn, but it is quite hard to play well, calling as it does for a highly developed card sense and a first-class card memory.

HOW TO PLAY

The Pinochle deck consists of forty-eight cards, made up of two full packs from which the eights to the twos have been removed. Thus all the cards are duplicated in both rank and suit. Most good players insist that both packs should have identical backs.

The rank of the cards for each suit, including whichever suit happens to be trumps, is : ace (high), ten, king, queen, jack, nine (low).

There are two objectives during play. On the one hand the players try to capture tricks which contain high ranking cards with a points value. At the same time they score points for laying down certain combinations of cards known as 'melds'.

The values of cards won in tricks are as follows:

Each ace	11 points
Each ten	10 points
Each king	4 points
Each queen	3 points
Each jack	2 points
Nines	no score
For winning the last trick	10 points

The total number of points available from tricks during the play is 250.
The melds that can be made and their scoring values are:

Flush (ace, ten, king, queen, jack of trumps)	150 points
Royal marriage (king and queen of trumps)	40 points
Marriage (king and queen of any other suit)	20 points
'Hundred aces' (four aces of different suits)	100 points
'Eighty kings' (four kings of different suits)	80 points
'Sixty queens' (four queens of different suits)	60 points
'Forty jacks' (four jacks of different suits)	40 points
Pinochle (queen of spades and jack of diamonds)	40 points
Dix, pronounced 'deece', (nine of trumps)	10 points

Although every card is duplicated in Pinochle, no single hand can meld anything like all of the above combinations. Realistically, the best hands will score from melds about the total number of points that are available from the tricks and on many occasions the count for melds will be much less. At the same time, points from tricks will be split between the two players. The art of Pinochle lies in playing the cards in such a way as to reconcile the two ways of scoring and thereby achieve the highest possible combined total.

To start the game players cut for deal. Whoever cuts the higher card, according to the rank of the cards at Pinochle, becomes dealer. Thereafter the deal alternates from hand to hand.

The cards are dealt four at a time, four to the non-dealer, four to the dealer, until both players have twelve cards. The next card, at the top of the pack, is turned face up on the table. Its suit determines trumps for the deal. If the turned up card is a nine, the dealer immediately scores 10 points for exposing the dix. The remainder of the cards are the 'stock' pile from which the players draw during the game. They are placed face down next to the trump card.

The non-dealer selects any card from his hand and leads to the first trick. His opponent then plays a card to complete the trick. Each player keeps the tricks he has captured beside him on the table, separately from those won by his rival.

As long as there are cards in the stock, the play of the tricks differs in several respects from the usual rules for most games based on the trick-taking principle. As at Whist, a player is not required to win a trick even though he is able to do so, nor need he win by trumping if he cannot follow suit. But at Pinochle he is not compelled to follow suit at all, irrespective of whether the card led is in a side suit or a trump.

Bearing in mind, the duplication of the cards in the Pinochle deck, and that the ten ranks between the ace and the king, tricks can be won in one of three ways. Either player may win by playing the higher ranking card of the suit led. Or second player can trump a side suit lead whether or not he is able to follow suit, and so gain the trick. Finally, where two cards of identical rank and denomination are played, the card led wins the trick.

For example if the ten of clubs is led out and the other ten of clubs is played to it, the first ten takes the trick.

During the first phase of the deal, whilst the stock is available to replenish the hands, the player who wins a trick has the right to meld one of any of the combinations he may hold. After the winner of a trick has exercised his option of putting down on the table one of the melds he may hold, he draws a card from the stock, and when his opponent has done likewise he leads to the next trick. Melded cards on the table remain part of a player's hand and may be played to a trick at any time. So each player's hand always consists of twelve cards. However, cards won in tricks are buried until the final count and may not be referred to during the play. The process of taking tricks and melding continues until one card alone remains face down in the stock. No more melds are permitted and the first stage of the deal is over. Players may not look at the cards whilst they are still in the stock, but it is permitted to count the number left there in order to ascertain how many tricks are still to be played before the melding phase is due to end.

Melding is subject to a set of rules that require a thorough explanation. These rules are straightforward enough, provided they are taken in logical order and one step at a time.

i) Only the winner of a trick may meld and the meld must be laid face up on the table before a fresh card is taken from the stock.

ii) Only one meld may be made per trick, and so a player holding more than one meld must go on to win further tricks to enable him to declare them separately and so score for them. It often happens that a player has one or more potential scoring combinations in his hand near the end of the first stage of play before the stock is exhausted. If he cannot win the tricks necessary to meld them in the correct way, he does not score for them.

iii) The exception to this rule for melding is the dix. After he has won a trick, a player who holds the nine of trumps may exchange it for the turned up trump card on the table and score 10 points for so doing. He may *also* meld a combination from his hand, should he have one, without first winning another trick. He would then score 10 for the dix *plus* the value of his meld. The exchanged turn-up card can itself be used to achieve this double score. Thus if the queen of hearts is the turned up trump and a player has the nine and king of hearts, as soon as he wins a trick, he may exchange the nine for the queen and immediately lay down the royal marriage for a total of 10+40 = 50 points.

iv) The second nine of trumps may also be used to score 10 points after its holder has won a trick. In this case it is merely exhibited in order to claim the points, and again another meld may be laid down at the same turn. If however the dix is used to play directly to a trick without having first been melded in the proper way, it does not score.

v) A single card may be used in two or more melds, provided they are of different classes. For example, a queen of spades may form part of four queens, pinochle and a marriage for scores of 60, 40 and 20 (40 for a royal marriage), provided she is laid down in accordance with the other rules of melding. However if say, a pinochle has already been melded, it is not permitted to simply add another jack of diamonds to the queen of spades on the table and receive credit for a second pinochle. The queen has been used for one pinochle and the rule is that it may only score again in a different type of meld. To score for another pinochle, both the second queen of spades and the second jack of diamonds would have to be declared as a separate meld.

This applies to all combinations but comes into play most often in the case of marriages. Suppose a player puts out the king and queen of clubs and claims 20 for a marriage. He may not later add another king of clubs to the melded queen for a second marriage. Again he must meld the duplicate king and queen to gain the points for the other marriage in clubs. Since the cards already melded may be subsequently played off in tricks, care must be taken to remember of which melds any cards remaining on the table were originally a part. Otherwise the rules of melding may be broken. Say a player has melded four kings and a marriage in clubs. He later plays the queen of clubs to a trick, leaving the king of the suit on the table as part of the melded kings. The queen has disappeared but the king still cannot be used for a second club marriage.

vi) Although as we have seen, a card on the table can be converted into a new meld of a different class by adding further cards to it, this is only allowed if at least one card is played from hand. Thus a player is not permitted to simply move already melded cards around on the table to gain extra points. Furthermore, if one card from hand simultaneously forms part of two combinations, only the most valuable scores. For example, should a player have a pinochle already melded and later meld four kings, he would score 'Eighty kings' but nothing for the spade marriage. As explained, he could not later move the queen of spades from the pinochle up to the king and claim a marriage.

vii) Of all the possible melds, only a flush has two scoring combinations within it: the flush itself and a royal marriage. Here the rule is that if the ace, ten, king, queen, and jack of trumps are laid down simultaneously, the melder scores only 150 for the flush and not 40 extra for a royal marriage. On the other hand if he first melds the king and queen of trumps, scoring 40 for royal marriage, he may later add the ace, ten and jack of the suit, and gain another 150 for the completed flush.

viii) A combination of four kings of different suits and four different queens is known as a 'roundhouse' or 'around the world'. In many games of the Pinochle family this attracts a score of 240 (80 for kings, 60 for queens, 40 for a royal marriage plus 60 for the other marriages). In some schools the 240 for a roundhouse is played at two-handed Pinochle, provided all eight cards are declared simultaneously. However this would offend most purists of the game, for it breaks all the rules of melding. Separate melding in the proper way allows a maximum of only 220 from four kings and four queens. This total might be made up of four kings for 80, to which three queens including the queen of trumps are later added separately for a further 80 from marriages. Then the final queen is laid down to score 'Sixty queens' but nothing for the fourth marriage. This gives a grand total of 220 points, the strictly proper maximum for this combination of cards in the two-handed game.

ix) The final opportunity to meld belongs to the player who wins the trick immediately prior to the appearance of the last card in the stock. Once the stock is exhausted, and the final card and the exposed trump have been drawn, no further melds can be made.

After the melding phase is over, the player who wins the trick and picks up the last stock card must show it to his opponent before taking it into his hand. The opponent picks up the exposed trump which will usually be the dix that has been exchanged for a higher trump. Any melded cards remaining on the table are also taken into the hands, so that each player still has twelve cards. These final twelve cards are played off in tricks. The player who won the trick before the stock was exhausted leads, but in this closing phase of the game different rules for the play of tricks apply.

Now the players must follow suit if they are able. They need not win a trick in a side suit should they choose not to, but if they cannot follow suit and hold a trump, they must play it and so win the trick. Only when they cannot follow *and* have no trump can they discard from some other suit. If trumps are led, the second player must win the trick by playing a higher trump if he can. If he cannot play a higher trump, he must follow with a lower one and may only discard from another suit should he have no trumps left.

The scoring of a hand is in two stages. Points from melds are added to each player's score as they are made in play. Points won in tricks are counted when the whole hand has been completed. The values of cards won in tricks are given in the table set out earlier, but it is a convention of the game to score for tricks in multiples of ten. Only seven, eight and nine are rounded up, so a player scoring a total of 126 from tricks would receive only 120 points, but with a total of 127, 128 or 129, he gets 130 points. The winner of the very last trick of the whole deal scores 10 points.

The game is won by the first player to score 1000 points from a series of deals. If both players reach 1000 on the same deal, the one with the higher score wins. In this circumstance, however, or in the rare event of a tie, some players agree to play on to 1250, 1500, 1750 and so on until a clear result is obtained.

Some players use the 'call-out' to establish a winner. If at any time during the hand, but not after the last trick of the deal has been played, either player believes he has reached 1000, he may claim the game. Such a claim, or call-out, can only be made after the player has won a trick. The deal is ended by the claim, and the scores from tricks are evaluated. If he is correct and has reached 1000, he wins the game even if his opponent is found to have a higher score. If however he is wrong and he has not in fact made 1000 at the time that he called, he loses no matter what score his opponent has accumulated.

In games where one player has a good lead and needs only a few points from tricks to reach 1000, the call-out is a safe way of establishing a win. Should the game be very close however, it requires extremely accurate counting during play, not only of a player's own trick score but also that of his opponent. In Pinochle, play is fairly rapid and close calls are best left to the expert player.

In the event of neither player being confident enough to call at 1000 and both reaching that score on the same deal, the game continues to 1250, 1500, 1750, etc., and only ends when a player successfully calls game or when a clear winner emerges at one of these scores.

The use of the call-out is strictly optional, but it is an accepted part of the American game at the most advanced level. To prevent misunderstandings it must be mutually agreed upon before play starts.

The score can be recorded on paper or by the use of chips. When chips are used, each player takes counters worth the number of points in a complete game, that is 1000. Every time a player scores he transfers the appropriate number of chips from a right-hand pile to one on his left. When all the chips have been exhausted in the right-hand pile, he has reached the game score of 1000. In games which go beyond 1000 to 1250 etc., all the chips are put back into the pile on the right and again transferred to the left until a winner is established.

THE PLAY OF A HAND

This hand played between Mary and Bill shows the full play of the twenty-four tricks of a Pinochle deal. A close study of the sequence should elucidate any points about the mechanics of the game which may be in doubt. For the sake of clarity it is set out in tabular form.

Mary is the dealer, so it is Bill who leads to the first trick.

Mary (dealer): ♣K Q ◇ A 10 K J J 9 ♠A K ♡J 9

Bill: ♣Q J J 9 ◇10 Q Q ♠Q Q J ♡A J

Turned up trump: ♣10

Mary				Bill		
draws	melds	plays		plays	melds	draws
				◇Q		
		◇10				
	♣KQ (40 pts)	(Mary's trick)				
♣A						♡10
		♡9				
				♡10		
				(Bill's trick)	Exchanges dix for ♣10 (10 pts)	
◇9						♡9
				♡9		
		◇9		(Bill's trick)		
♣K						♣A

Mary				Bill		
draws	melds	plays		plays	melds	draws
				♠Q		
		◇9		(Bill's trick)		
♠A						♡Q
				♣J		
		♣K (From table)				
		(Mary's trick)				
♡K						♠9
		♡J				
				♡A		
				(Bill's trick)	♣Q◇Q ♠Q♡Q (60 pts)	
♣9						♡A
				♠9		
		♠A				
	Exhibits dix (10 pts)	(Mary's trick)				
	♣K◇K ♠K♡K (80 pts)					
♡10						♠10
		◇J				
				◇10		
				(Bill's trick)		
♠K						♥K

Mary				Bill		
draws	melds	plays		plays	melds	draws
				◇Q (From table)		
		◇K (From table)				
		(Mary's trick)				
♣10						◇K
		♣K				
				♣10		
				(Bill's trick)	♡K to ♡Q on table (20 pts)	
♠9						♡Q
				♡Q (From table)		
		♡10				
		(Mary's trick)				
♠10						◇A
		♣A				
		(Mary's trick)		♠J		
♠J (Shown to Bill)						♣9 (From table)

The stock is now exhausted and the hands are:

Mary: ♣10 K Q 9 ◇A J ♠A 10 K J 9 ♡K

Bill: ♠A 10 Q J 9 ◇A K ♣Q ♡A K Q J

Mary	Bill
plays	plays
♠A	
(Mary's trick)	♠Q
♠9	
	♣9
	(Bill's trick)
	♡A
♡K	(Bill's trick)
	♡J
♣9	
(Mary's trick)	
♠J	
	♣J
	(Bill's trick)
	♡Q
♣Q	
(Mary's trick)	

Mary		Bill
plays		plays
♠ K		
		♣ Q
		(Bill's trick)
		♣ A
♣ K		(Bill's trick)
		♣ 10
♣ 10		(Bill's trick)
		♡ K
♠ 10		(Bill's trick)
		♢ A
♢ J		(Bill's trick)
		♢ K
♢ A		
(Mary's trick)		
(Last trick 10 pts)		

The scores are:

Mary			**Bill**		
Melds (added on as scored)			Melds (added on as scored)		
40+10+80		= 130	10+60+20		= 90
Tricks			Tricks		
4 aces	44		4 aces	44	
2 tens	20		6 tens	60	
3 kings	12		5 kings	20	
6 queens	18		2 queens	6	
3 jacks	6		5 jacks	10	
last trick	10			140	140
	110	110			230
		240			

So this was a fairly even hand. Mary came out best in melds but Bill had the better trumps after the stock was cleared, which enabled him to make up most of the deficit by utilising them to win the majority of the last twelve tricks.

HINTS ON PLAY

Memory is a vital part of Pinochle. The best players know the exact contents of the opposing hand the moment the last card in the stock is exposed. For the beginner such a feat of memory may seem rather daunting. An accurate card memory only comes as a result of application and long practice, but even beginners should at least make a point of counting trumps and of knowing how many aces are left to be played. With this knowledge they will find the handling of the last twelve tricks relatively straightforward, and it is the play of these tricks which often makes the difference between a reasonable score and a good one.

In the early stages of a deal, players should try to keep open as many options as possible for potential melds. However it is not possible to save everything and the better the hand, the more choices there will be between what to keep and what to play off in tricks. When likely scoring combinations have to be broken up, it is best to start from the jacks and work upwards. As play proceeds, by carefully watching which cards the opponent puts down, it will be apparent what melds have become impossible and clues can be found as to which are unlikely. So if one player wins a trick early on with the ten of trumps, it is probable (but not certain!) that his rival will never be able to complete a flush during the deal. The chances are that the ten was played from both tens of the trump suit.

Players should not worry too much about conceding cheap tricks early on. Forming a good hand which will score well for melds is much more important. So playing nines and jacks to the opening tricks does little harm. Tens are not part of any scoring combination except in trumps and are most useful for capturing a trick when a player wishes to meld. Even the lead of a ten may win an early trick, for to take it, the opponent must give up an ace or a trump and thereby perhaps reduce his chances of a 'Hundred aces' or a flush.

Sometimes there will be a choice of what to meld and how. Much depends on the stage the hand has reached. Obviously with the stock nearly exhausted, a flush must be melded entire and the royal marriage foregone, unless its holder is absolutely sure of being able to win another trick to ensure the double score. A player having four aces at any stage, should meld them at once. As soon as they are on the table and scored for, they can be used to take tricks. Unmelded in the hand, they are useless. Holding more than one meld and with plenty of time to win tricks, the rule is to first lay down the one which has in it the least number of cards that are to be saved for future scores. So from a hand of jack of clubs, spades and diamonds, queen of spades and king of spades, a player who has given up hope of getting four kings should meld the marriage first. This makes the king immediately available for play to a trick. If the pinochle is melded first, the queen must remain on the table until the marriage can be declared, and the jack of diamonds has to stay there too in case the jack of hearts comes along to make forty jacks.

It is small points like these that make the difference between a good Pinochle player and an indifferent one. Giving information away unnecessarily is another area of the game where beginners often fall down. So if a marriage has already been melded and a player has the duplicate king in hand, wishing to play a king, he should always choose the one from the table. Why tell his opponent that the second king is unavailable? The latter may be saving for four kings and might go on doing so until the bitter end, so long as he is uncertain of the whereabouts of the second king.

Near the close of the melding phase it pays to win as many tricks as possible, if only because the more cards that have been drawn, the more likely is the opponent to have formed high scoring melds. Defence against a possible flush is most important. The correct play is to lead trumps. In order to win the trick necessary to meld, the opponent may well have no alternative but to use a trump from the flush itself and so lose the 150 score.

In the play of tricks generally, given a choice, the best leads are from the longest suit in hand. One player's long suit could well be his opponent's short one. The latter may have to waste valuable trumps very quickly in order to win the tricks he needs to declare his melds.

Trump superiority is usually the decisive factor during the last twelve tricks. So again it pays to go on leading from the longest suit and try to force the opponent to trump. If he had the majority of trumps at the start, he will not want to use them up in this way and possibly lose control of the final few tricks. For the same reason, unless a player has by far and away the best and longest trumps, it seldom pays to begin by drawing them. Should a player have no trumps left for the end play, he may well lose tricks unnecessarily, including the 10 points for the last trick of all.

Experience is the most valuable asset at Pinochle. It would be wrong to expect to become an expert overnight, but given the right approach and the desire to succeed, it is possible to reach a fair standard at the game within a reasonably short period of time.

To many English eyes Pinochle may seem a strange amalgam of several major games where the rules of each are tampered with in a rather peculiar way. Be that as it may, Pinochle has a big following in the United States and is one of the most entertaining card games regularly played by Americans.

AUCTION PINOCHLE

Pinochle is basically a two-handed game. It is in fact possible to play three- or four-handed, but these versions are in the main unsatisfactory. So when more than two Pinochle players sit down to their favourite game, it is usual to play a variant which incorporates the element of bidding. Auction Pinochle, even more than the parent game, is subject to wide differences in playing conventions. It is a gambling game and like all money games, it defies any attempt to codify its laws. The game described below is the one generally recognised as standard in the card clubs of the great metropolitan centres of the U.S., even if there are slight variations from place to place.

HOW TO PLAY

There are three hands in Auction, although four or even five may sit in on a session. When four play, the dealer is inactive for one round. With five participants neither the dealer nor the second player to his left receive any cards.

The game is played with the forty-eight card deck described for Pinochle, and the rank of the cards, the points scored for melds and the value of cards won in tricks are exactly the same as in straight Pinochle.

The idea is for each player to bid what score he believes he can accumulate from melds and tricks. The player who makes the highest numerical bid becomes the 'bidder' and his two opponents play together to try to prevent him achieving the total he has nominated.

Each active player receives fifteen cards. Beginning with the player to the dealer's immediate left, the cards are dealt in batches of three according to a 3-3-3-3-3 or a 4-4-4-3 pattern, whichever the dealer prefers. After the first round of the deal, three cards are dealt face down on the table to form what is known as the 'widow'. So all forty-eight cards in the game are immediately in play.

The bidding goes as follows. Again starting with the player on the left of the dealer and moving round the table, each has the option of bidding or passing. Bids are made in multiples of ten but at this stage no suits are mentioned as possible trumps. Players may subsequently raise their bids in an effort to win the call. Once a player has passed however, he may not bid again. When two players have passed, the auction is over and the remaining player, who has made the highest call, becomes bidder for the deal.

In a game without official laws there is a multiplicity of bidding conventions, but nowadays most schools insist that the player at the dealer's left must make a minimum bid of 300. He may of course bid more if he chooses but whatever the contents of his hand, he must call at least '300'. It is then up to the other two players to decide whether they wish to better the bid or pass.

When it has been established who shall play as bidder, that player exposes the widow and gives his opponents the chance to examine it. Next he takes the three cards in the widow into his hand. From the eighteen cards he now holds, he lays down as many melds as he can. In Auction players do not have to win tricks before making melds. The bidder must in fact lay down all he wishes to score for in melds before he leads to the first trick.

However the basic rules of melding itself remain the same as in straight Pinochle. A single card can be used as part of any number of melds, provided they are of different types. So the queen of spades can be melded as part of a flush, of four queens and of a pinochle for a score of $150 + 60 + 40 = 250$ points. However, to score for a second pinochle, it is not sufficient to merely attach another jack of diamonds to the melded queen. As in straight Pinochle, a player must lay down both the duplicate jack and the other queen of spades to get a further 40 points for pinochle. Only 150 are scored for a flush. A royal marriage can score for 40 only if it is laid down separately and not as part of a flush.

Both dixes can be melded for 10 points each.

If the bidder declares four kings of different suits and four different queens, he receives 240 for a 'roundhouse', made up of 80 for the kings, 60 for the queens and $40 + 20 + 20 + 20$ for a royal marriage and three ordinary marriages. However, if a flush is laid down at the same time, the roundhouse is worth only 200, because the royal marriage does not score. So the grand total for a flush and a roundhouse is $150 + 200 = 350$ points. On the other hand if a flush in diamonds is melded with a roundhouse, the score goes to 390 because the pinochle meld adds an extra 40 points.

The melding of a flush or of a royal marriage automatically fixes the trump suit for the subsequent play of the tricks.

It is a generally accepted rule of Auction that if the bidder is not completely happy with the arrangement of his melds, he may change it at any time before he leads to the first trick. This means that he can also change the trump suit by rearranging the pattern of any flushes or royal marriages with other cards from his hand. Clearly however, he must eventually make up his mind. It is the arrangement of the cards immediately before he picks them up from the table and plays to the opening trick that determines his final score for melds, and the trump suit when he has melded a flush or a royal marriage.

Sometimes the bidder, having looked at the widow and considered the full scoring potential of his hand, may decide he has overbid to such an extent that, even if the game proceeds to the play of the tricks, he has no chance of making his call. In this circumstance he can concede defeat and is said to lose 'single bete', pronounced 'bate'. In hopeless cases such a concession is well worth making, for, as we shall see, it affects the rate at which an unsuccessful bidder pays his opponents. The bidder may concede at any time during the deal, but in order to claim the advantages of single bete he must do so before he plays a card to the first trick.

Similarly, the bidder's opponents may concede that he is certain to make his call. In this case they may concede the bid at any time before the beginning of the trick play or indeed at any point afterwards. However the concession of one opponent is not binding on the other. Both have to agree to a concession before the bidder can claim his stakes.

Since in Auction it is not necessary to win even a single trick to receive full credit for melded cards, the bidder may be able to make his call from melds alone. In this case, as with single bete, the tricks are not played for.

When however, as usually happens, the bidder does need points from tricks to achieve his bid, and there is no concession from either side, he now 'buries' three cards from his hand to reduce it to the fifteen cards required for the final phase of the deal. He may only bury cards which have not been melded and he places his three discards face down on the table without showing them to his opponents. If he buries a trump or trumps from his hand however, he must inform the other players of their number, but not their denomination. The point of this rule is that a careful count of trumps in play is often decisive in determining how the opponents will defend against the bid. A buried trump, if undisclosed, would almost certainly confuse them and give the bidder an unfair advantage. Of course other cards, especially aces, can have a vital influence on the tricks, but in their case the bidder need not make any announcement about what he is burying.

The fifteen tricks are played out according to the following rules:

i) If he has not already done so by melding a flush or royal marriage, the bidder nominates the suit he wishes to be trumps.

ii) The bidder leads to the first trick. Thereafter the winner of one trick leads to the next.

iii) Players must follow in a side suit if they can, but they are not compelled to try to win the trick.

iv) A player who cannot follow in a side suit must play a trump if he has one. Only if he has no trumps in his hand may he discard from some other suit.

v) If a card in a side suit is led and the second player trumps, the third player must also play a trump if he cannot follow suit, but he need not play a higher trump and thus overtrump second player.

vi) When a trump is led however, each player must, if able, play a higher trump than the highest one already played. This rule applies even if one opponent to the bidder is forced to better a card played by the other which has already won the trick.

vii) A trick is won by the highest trump contained in it or, if it contains no trump, by the highest card played of the suit led. When two cards of the same rank and suit form part of the same trick, the card played first wins, provided of course the third card is a lower one.

viii) Should the bidder win the final trick, he scores 10 points for doing so.

When the tricks have been completed, the bidder adds up the points accumulated from his melds and from the scoring cards won in tricks. Provided he has won at least one trick, he also scores for any cards of value contained in the three he buried. If the total equals or exceeds his bid, he has made his call and is paid by the others in the game. Should the total fall short of the bid, however, the bidder is said to be defeated 'double bete' and must settle at a higher rate than if he had conceded for single bete.

Stakes are settled after each deal. Pen and paper may be used to record the score but it is more usual to pay in chips distributed to the players before the beginning of the game.

The value of bids varies widely from school to school, but the following scale would attract a reasonable consensus. As in straight Pinochle, odd points from tricks are rounded up to the next ten only if the total ends in a seven, eight or nine.

300–340 points	3 units
350–390 points	5 units
400–440 points	10 units
450–490 points	15 units
500–540 points	20 units
550–590 points	25 units
600–640 points	30 units
650–690 points	35 units
700 points or more	40 units

Scores of just over 700 are technically possible, but in practice any successful call of even 600 or more is rare.

The settlement of stakes is regulated by the following rules:

i) If the bidder is successful in his call, he receives the value of his bid according to the above table from all participants in the game, including any players who were inactive on the deal. If he made spades trumps, he is paid out at double stakes.

ii) If the bidder is defeated in his call single bete, that is he conceded before leading to the first trick, he pays all players, including inactive ones, the value of his bid at single stakes. Again these are doubled if spades were trumps.

iii) If the bidder is defeated double bete, that is he led to the first trick and later conceded the hopelessness of his bid or failed to make it, he pays all participants including inactive ones at double stakes, and at four times the basic value of his bid if spades were trumps.

It is usual, but not compulsory, to play Auction Pinochle with a kitty. Here again there are wide divergences in practice but the game described below makes a sensible one on which most players would agree.

Before the first hand every participant 'antes' the value of the minimum bid (3 units) into the kitty. They make a similar ante each time a hand is passed by all three active players and there is a redeal.

The kitty neither pays to the bidder nor collects from him on bids up to 340 points inclusive. On bids of 350 or more the kitty functions exactly as if it were a player, that is it pays or collects single bete, double bete and twice the rate for bids in spades depending on the outcome of the call.

In some schools, however, the kitty collects at the prevailing rate on all unsuccessful bids of 350 plus, but the first bidder to make a call of 350 or over scoops the pool and takes the whole of the accumulated stakes in the kitty.

When the player to the left of the dealer makes the forced minimum bid of 300 and becomes the bidder, he may pass without looking at the widow. In this case he pays the value of this minimum bid to the kitty, but nothing to any of the participants in the game. If however he decides to look at the widow, he is deemed to have accepted the bid and is subject to the normal rules of play and payment.

If at any time the kitty is unable to pay a successful bidder in full, all those in the game, including any inactive on the deal, must each contribute an equal amount to the kitty to enable it to meet its obligations.

If at the end of a deal the kitty has nothing in it, it must be replenished by each participant contributing an ante equal to the value of the minimum bid.

At the end of the game any stakes remaining in the kitty are divided equally among all those participating.

THE PLAY OF A HAND

Bill, Mary, Paul and Jane are playing Auction Pinochle. Bill is the dealer and receives no cards. The player at Bill's left is Mary who has been dealt this hand:

♠10 J 9   ◇10 10 K K Q J   ♣10 10 K   ♡K J 9

Mary has good diamonds as a trump suit, but is missing the ace of the suit and can only meld a royal marriage with no other scoring combinations in her hand. Even if the widow comes up with the ace of diamonds, she has no real prospect of succeeding in a call. However, as player to the dealer's left, she must make the minimum bid of 300.

Paul has a much better hand:

♠A 10 K Q J 9   ◇J 9 9   ♣K Q Q J 9   ♡J

A flush with the dix, four jacks, a pinochle and an ordinary marriage in clubs adds up to a certain 260 in melds. The problem is that the hand is not all that strong in trick-taking potential. Even the trumps, despite their length, are not especially good. On the other hand should the widow hold an ace or two, or a couple of trumps, a not too ambitious bid could well succeed. If it fails, it will be expensive, for spades will be trumps and that means double stakes. However with 260 in the bag and all to play for, Paul decides to bid '310'.

Jane who is last to bid also has a good hand:

♠A K Q   ◇A A Q   ♣A A 9   ♡A 10 10 K Q 9

Here there are a 'Hundred aces' and good hearts for trumps with a royal marriage and the dix, as well as a marriage in spades. Even without any help from the widow Jane can meld 170, and all those aces and strong trumps should ensure that any reasonable bid will succeed. However Jane is not the sort to get carried away. She betters Paul's call by just 10 and bids '320'.

Mary, with her forced opening bid on a poor hand heaves a sigh of relief and passes. Paul considers for a moment whether to risk another bid but the fact that he must make spades trumps finally brings him down, quite rightly, on the side of caution. He too passes.

Jane is the bidder, and must now expose the widow which is:

♣J   ♡A Q

These cards are very useful indeed. Jane's melds are not improved, but the ace of hearts and another heart must surely prove decisive. No question of a concession here. She melds her 170 making hearts trumps, and buries the jack and nine of clubs and queen of diamonds. This means that Jane will be in a very powerful position when it comes to the play of the hands.

The hands are now:

Jane (to lead):

♡A A 10 10 K Q Q 9 ♠AKQ ◇A A ♣A A

Mary:

♡K J 9 ♠10 J 9 ◇10 10 K K Q J ♣10 10 K

Paul:

♡J ♠A 10 K Q J 9 ◇J 9 9 ♣K Q Q J 9

Normally it is a dangerous tactic to draw trumps too soon, but Jane has eight of the twelve and they include both aces and both tens. She can afford to pull the four trumps in her opponents' hands and will then be able to cash her aces with no risk of having them trumped. This is how she plays. She then gives up two spade tricks, losing her king and queen to Paul's ace and ten. Mary's ten and jack of spades are also included in these two tricks. However Paul now plays, Jane has nothing left but trumps and must win the remaining tricks, catching all the points-scoring cards from the other two hands and scoring 10 points for the very last trick.

Jane has achieved a wonderful haul of scoring cards from the tricks.. With her buried cards she has seven aces, six tens, seven kings, seven queens and seven jacks plus 10 for the final trick for a total from tricks of 210 points. Jane melded 170 points, so with her trick total of 210 she has made a score of 380 which is well in excess of her bid of 320. At first sight she appears to have undercalled her hand. More adventurous players might well have made a higher bid, but the two good trumps in the widow were an unexpected piece of luck that converted a good hand into a much better one. For her bid of 320 she gets 3 units from each player, including Bill who was the inactive dealer. Because her bid was less than 350 she collects nothing from the kitty.

HINTS ON PLAY

Auction Pinochle is without doubt one of the best of all games for three hands. Every aspect of card technique needs to be mastered in order to play the game to a high standard. When to bid? How much to bid? When to concede and when to play? How to play the cards to the best advantage? The beginner is immediately confronted with a whole range of complex problems.

There are no straightforward solutions. Successful bidding requires a delicate blend of the kind of precise estimate of chances which characterises the accomplished Bridge player, and the near second sight which only the finest Poker players seem to possess. The trick-taking phase of the game, either as bidder or as one of his opponents, calls for a thorough mastery of the principles of Whist play. What follows is only the merest summary of the main features of good practice, but if it lays the foundations of sound basic technique for someone starting in what is a very difficult game, it will have achieved its aims.

It helps in deciding what to bid if the beginner fully understands the types of call that are open to him. First, there is the safety bid. This is arrived at by counting up what points can be scored from the melds that are already held in hand. Little or no help is asssumed from the widow, and only points that are certain to accrue from tricks are added on, with a pessimistic view of scoring cards that can be captured from the opponents.

Then there is the risk bid. Here the player assumes a reasonable amount of assistance from the widow either to improve the existing value of his melds or to strengthen his hand for the play of the tricks. In addition, the most favourable view is taken of valuable cards that can be won from the enemy hands.

Finally a player may bluff. Here he makes a bid in the knowledge that he has no chance of making his call. The object is to force an opponent to overbid his hand to the point where he subsequently fails in his bid.

Bluffing is definitely not for the novice, because against experienced players the bluffer may well find himself left in a hopeless bid, and this will prove very expensive. At the same time no one ever wins consistently at Auction by sticking to safe bids alone. In practice cast-iron hands that are certain to succeed come along rarely, and only by taking calculated risks can a player hope to keep regularly ahead of the game. This means that on nine hands out of ten some help from the widow must be assumed. The problem is to decide how much. Pure chance enters the picture here, but there are certain guidelines which can help in calculating the possibilities.

The following table gives the odds against finding a specific card in the three blind cards of the widow, assuming that the hand contains neither of the required duplicate cards of a given suit and rank.

Open Places	**approximate odds**
1	5–1 against
2	2–1 against
3	evens
4	3–2 on
5	2–1 on

So if a player holds ace, ten, king, queen in a potential trump suit, it is 5–1 against him drawing a jack of the suit from the widow to complete a flush. If he has king and queen of diamonds, queen of hearts and queen of clubs, the odds are evens that he will pick up either queen of spades, king of hearts or king of clubs to improve his score from melds. With five places open, for example having queen of spades, queen of diamonds and queen of clubs only, it is 2–1 on that the widow will improve the hand by supplying one of jack of diamonds for a pinochle, queen of hearts for sixty queens or a king to match one of the three queens in hand to complete a marriage.

A knowledge of these mathematical chances can on occasion prove useful, but they take no account of how the trick-taking potential of a hand can be enhanced by the widow. In fact this cannot be calculated mathematically with any degree of accuracy. In practice seasoned players find it convenient to assume that the widow will provide an extra 20 to 30 points from melds and tricks combined. This seems very little. It could well be much more from time to time, but a player who makes a regular habit of overestimating the possibilities of the widow will nearly always be disappointed.

When to concede and when to play is frequently the most difficult decision of all. Basically the bidder looks at his score from melds, adds the value of buried cards, counts his certain winners from trumps, aces and any guarded tens, and deducts the resulting total from the points value of his bid. He must now try to estimate whether the shortfall can be made up from the opponents' ranking cards which will fall to his sure winners, and from any cards in his hand that are not bound to win tricks but which may do so. For the best players this may involve abstruse calculations quite beyond the scope of this book. In the main, however, experience will teach the proficient player to make a reasonably accurate estimate of how many points he is likely to accumulate from tricks.

Even if a player decides that he is likely to fail in his bid by a few points, this does not mean that he should automatically concede. In general, unless the situation is obviously hopeless, it pays to play rather than concede on borderline hands, and to take an optimistic view about winning problematical cards in the trick play. The mathematics of single and double bete in regard to the rate of payment are such that even if the bidder believes the odds are against him succeeding in his call, he should play on. In fact only if the odds are 2–1 or worse should he concede. When spades are trumps however, having to play at double stakes means that he should not continue unless he gives himself at least an even chance of making his bid.

There are a number of possible strategies for burying cards and for the play of the tricks, depending on the make-up of given hands, but the following hints should help the beginner with the most common types of deal.

When considering what to bury, the longest suit outside trumps should nearly always be retained intact. Suits of three cards or less, especially if they contain intermediate cards likely to be lost in the tricks, make good discards, for it might well be possible to capture an ace or some other valuable card by trumping when the unsuspecting opponents begin the suit. If, on the other hand, a side suit holding is reduced to a singleton ace, it must be led immediately. Otherwise, when the opponents play their ace of the suit first, it will be lost. Tens, unsupported by other top cards, are very vulnerable in play and should be buried for a certain 10 points.

In the play of the tricks many beginners always start by drawing trumps. This is usually a mistake for either side, but it is particularly dangerous for the bidder unless he begins with overwhelming trump superiority in both length and strength. If the opponents can come to even a slight advantage in trumps, the bidder may lose control of the final stages of the deal, and being unable to regain the lead, he will be forced to throw valuable cards under established winners in the two enemy hands. There is one exception for the defending side to the general rule of not drawing trumps: when the bidder appears to be just a few points short of his bid. Then the opponents should lead trumps at him to try to stop him picking up points by using small trumps to win tricks in side suits where he is void.

In general it should be remembered that at Auction, as in all three-handed trick-taking games, the bidder is most vulnerable from the opponent to his right. Right-hand opponent leads through him up to his partner, and so threatens the intermediate cards in the bidder's hand. When left-hand opponent is on lead, the bidder goes last and has much greater freedom of manoeuvre in deciding what to play.

Counting points won in tricks during play is just as important in Auction as in the parent game. The beginner simply sets off in the hope of winning as many tricks as possible, often without thinking out what line of play is most likely to succeed, and lacks the flexibility to adapt his tactics to the developing situation. A knowledge of the exact number of points required to make a call after each trick can often enable the skilful exponent of the game to see a way of giving himself the very best chance of succeeding. This may mean modifying a much riskier strategy which seemed desirable earlier on. The object of the game is only to make the bid and there are no rewards for any extra points won above it. Likewise the opponents will be in a position to determine the best line of defence at any given time if they are aware of the precise state of the score.

PARTNERSHIP AUCTION PINOCHLE

Often when four join in a social game, Auction Pinochle is played with partners, two against two. The varieties of Partnership Auction are legion. Some use a regular Pinochle deck of forty-eight cards; others play with two or even three decks. Sometimes the game is played with a widow, sometimes without. Depending on how many cards are used and the variant being played, there can be bonuses for double, triple or quadruple melds. Bidding conventions and scoring systems diverge widely from game to game and from company to company. Clearly in a book of this scope it would be impossible to deal with all or even some of these almost endless variations, but the version described below is one of the simpler forms. It is also one of the most popular.

The partners sit opposite one another at the table. The forty-eight card pack is used. Players cut for deal. The player who cuts the highest card becomes the dealer. Thereafter the deal moves in a clockwise direction round the table. Each player is dealt twelve cards, distributed in batches of three. There is no widow.

Beginning with the player at the left of the dealer, each has a single opportunity to bid or pass. So, unlike three-handed Auction, in this game a player may not raise his original bid in order to try to win the call, although obviously the partner bidding second may use his one chance to bid to overcall the other side. Bids are made in multiples of 10 with no trump suit mentioned. There is usually a minimum bid of 100.

The player who makes the highest bid becomes the bidder. This means that he and his partner have undertaken to score between them on the deal at least the value of his bid. If every player passes without making a bid, the deal moves on to the next player who redistributes the cards.

When the auction is over, the bidder names the trump suit. All four players then meld any scoring combinations they may hold. The rules for melding are exactly the same as in the standard form of Auction Pinochle. Partners must meld separately. They may not combine their cards to build up joint melds, but their separate melds are added together and a note made of the total for each partnership before the beginning of the trick play. In order to receive credit on the score sheet for melds, a partnership must win at least one trick in the play.

Each player now picks up his melded cards from the table and the final phase of the deal begins. The bidder leads to the first trick. Except that twelve rather than fifteen tricks are played, the rules for the play of tricks are the same as in three-handed Auction, with the side who wins the very last trick scoring 10 points for doing so.

The final trick completed, each partnership counts up the points it has jointly gained from scoring cards won in tricks, and adds these to the combined value of its melds.

If the bidder and his partner jointly make from melds and tricks a score at least equal to the bid, the points value of the call, not the number of points actually scored, is added to their running total towards game.

If however, the bidding side's combined score from melds and tricks falls short of the bid, the points value of the call is deducted from their running total towards game, and their score from melds and tricks is lost. Thus minus totals are possible, and are denoted by a circle around them on the score sheet when a partnership is said to be 'in the hole'.

The opponents to the bidding side, whether the bid succeeds or not, always score their combined points from melds and tricks, and these are added to their running total towards game.

The game is won by the first side to reach 1000 points. If both partnerships reach or pass 1000 during the same deal, the bidder's side wins, unless the rule described below is adopted.

Many schools allow the 'call-out' to determine the result of a close game, as in straight Pinochle. So a player may at any time after his side has just won a trick claim that it has reached 1000 points. Play ceases and the scores to that point are examined. If the claim is found to be correct, the side which made the call-out wins, even though the other partnership may have a higher score. If, on the other hand, the side that has called has not in fact reached 1000 at the time play stopped, it loses the game, whatever score the opposing partnership has achieved.

Many prefer to play the game with double melds that attract huge bonus scores. The additional melds which can be scored in one hand are:

Double flush	1500 points
All eight aces	1000 points
All eight kings	800 points
All eight queens	600 points
All eight jacks	400 points
Double pinochle	300 points

When these melds are allowed, it is usual for the game to be 1500 or even 2000 up. As before, the call-out is optional by prior agreement between the players.

Partnership Auction is a much more hit-and-miss affair than the three-handed version, for a great deal of guesswork is involved in the bidding where each partner has only a single call and there can be none of the exchange of information that occurs in Bridge. However, many American card players prefer the variants of Partnership Auction to standard two-handed Pinochle and three-handed Auction, if only because they offer excellent entertainment without calling for the exacting self-discipline and precision play needed to excel at the parent games.

SEVEN UP

Seven Up is almost identical to the old English game of All Fours. It came to America in the early 1700's and has been played ever since in the United States where it is also called High-Low-Jack or Old Sledge. It has been superseded by more modern games but still commands a following, and is important as a basic card game from which quite a number of local variants in America have developed.

HOW TO PLAY

The game is for two, three or four players. When four play, they may do so as individuals but it is more usual to have two partnerships with each partner sitting opposite the other at the table.

The standard fifty-two card pack is used and in each suit the cards rank as at Whist: ace (high), king, queen, jack, ten, nine, eight, seven, six, five, four, three, two (low).

The idea of Seven Up is to play for the highest trump, the lowest trump, the jack of trumps and for game which is decided by totalling the value of high cards won in tricks. The first player or side to collect 7 points is the winner.

Players cut for deal, and the player who cuts the highest ranking card becomes the dealer. Thereafter the right to deal moves clockwise round the table. Each player receives six cards, dealt three at a time. The dealer then turns up the top card of the undealt pack. This 'turn-up' proposes the trump suit for the round. Should it be a jack, the dealer immediately scores 1 point.

The eventual trump suit is on all counts the vital factor in the subsequent game. It will not necessarily be the suit of the turn-up and must be determined before actual play can begin. The procedure is as follows.

The player at the left of the dealer consults his hand and either says, 'I stand', that is he accepts the turn-up suit as trumps, or 'I beg', by which he passes the decision to the dealer.

If the player to the left of the dealer begs, the dealer may then 'take it'. This means he opts to have the original turn-up card's suit as trumps and must 'give one' to the left-hand player who scores 1 point for the 'gift'.

If, however, the dealer prefers to have some other suit as trumps, he says, 'I refuse the gift' and 'runs the cards'. To do this, he deals a batch of three more cards to each player including himself and turns up a fresh card from the top of the pack. Again, if it is a jack the dealer scores 1 point unless it is the same suit as the first rejected turn-up. So it is possible for the dealer to score a maximum of 2 points for two turned up jacks.

Should the new card, whatever its denomination, be of the same suit as the original turn-up, it is discarded and three more cards are run to each player. This process goes on until a new suit is eventually exposed from the top of the pack to decide trumps. Subject to the rule that the very last card in the deck cannot be used to make trumps, it sometimes happens that the whole pack is exhausted without a different suit to the original one being turned up. In that event the cards are gathered in, shuffled and then redealt by the same dealer.

The dialogue followed to determine trumps is exclusively between the dealer and the player at his left, and in games with more than two players none of the others may even look at their cards until the trump suit is fixed.

Trumps having been fixed in this way, the players now reduce their hands to six cards should it be necessary, that is if the cards have been run beyond the first six dealt. They have an entirely free choice of what to discard, and the rejected cards are laid face down on the table without being shown to any other player.

The player on the dealer's left makes the opening lead. The hand is played out in six tricks, each player putting out one card to a trick, with play moving round the table in the normal clockwise direction. There is no requirement for any player to try to win a trick should he choose not to, but all must adhere to the following rules.

If a trump is led at any stage, the others must also play a trump if they have one. Otherwise they may discard from some other suit. If a side suit is led, players may follow or trump, that is they may use a trump even if they can in fact follow suit. Only if they cannot either follow suit *or* trump may they discard from a third suit. A trick is won by the highest trump it contains, or should it contain no trump, by the highest ranking card played of the suit led. The winner of one trick leads to the next.

Four points are available to be won in play as follows:

High: 1 point for the highest trump played, scored by the player to whom it was originally dealt. (A turned up jack for which the dealer has already scored 1 point is not in play for the purpose of determining the highest trump 'played'. So if a jack was turned up and the ten was the highest ranking card played in the tricks, the ten would count as the highest trump.)

Low: 1 point for the lowest trump, scored by the player to whom it was originally dealt.

Jack: 1 point for capturing the jack of trumps in the tricks won in play.

Game: 1 point for game, scored by the player who amasses the greatest points total for high cards won in tricks. The values of high cards won in tricks are:

Each ten –	10
Each ace –	4
Each king –	3
Each queen –	2
Each jack –	1

In the older English form of Seven Up, when there is a tie for game, it is customary to award 1 point to the non-dealer in a two-handed deal. However, since this is in effect a point for nothing, in the modern American tradition no point for game is scored by either side when more than one player has the same total from high cards captured in tricks.

Should there be only one trump in play, its original holder scores 2 points for both high and low; but if the single trump happens to be a jack, the third point goes to whoever captures it in a trick.

The player or side who first reaches a total of 7 points is the winner. If more than one player or side reach 7 on the same deal, the points are counted in this order: turned up jack, high, low, jack won in a trick, game. So there can be no tie in the final reckoning. Note that the dealer must refuse gift when his left-hand opponent, having already scored 6, begs. If the dealer 'gives one', he would automatically concede game.

Scores are kept with pen and paper. Alternatively, each player or side takes seven chips before the game begins, and reduces the pile by one every time a point is scored. Obviously whoever puts aside all his chips first is 'seven up' and wins the game.

There is one final rule which is of considerable importance in Seven Up. This concerns the circumstances of, and the penalty for, a revoke. A player is guilty of a revoke if he fails to play a trump to a trump lead when in fact he has a trump in his hand. There is also a revoke where a card is led in a side suit and a player discards from some third suit when he could follow or trump. A revoke is established when any player leads the first card to the next trick. Before that, a player who has played incorrectly can withdraw his illegal card and all those who have played after him may take back their cards; after the next trick has been led to, the revoke is a *fait accompli* and the tricks are played out to the end.

The penalty for a revoke is harsh. The player who revokes must allow each of his opponents, or the opposing side in a partnership game, to add 1 point to their score if the jack is not in play and 2 points if it is. For this purpose, a turned up jack is not in play, since it is not available to be captured in a trick. In addition the player or side who has revoked may not count for jack or game. On the other hand the points for a turned up jack, and for high and low, are not affected by a revoke and may be scored for by an offending player or side.

THE PLAY OF A HAND

Seven Up is an easy game to learn but the following deal between Mary and Bill will elucidate any points about which the reader might not be absolutely clear.

| **Mary** (dealer) | **Bill** |
| (holding 4 points towards seven up) | (6 points towards seven up) |

♠J ◇K Q 3 ♣— ♡J 4   ♠A Q ◇A 5 ♣— ♡10 8

Turn-up: ♣5

Bill has quite a good hand which includes a ten of hearts with one guard that will count 10 towards game if he retains it in a trick he can capture. On the other hand he has no clubs, the trump suit proposed by the turn-up, so he has no alternative but to beg.

Mary now assesses her hand. This is also quite powerful given the fact that some of the cards higher than her court cards are probably in the undealt pack. However, she too has no clubs. She knows that Bill does not have many, or he would have accepted them as trumps. Does she take the clubs or run the cards? In fact there can be only one decision. Bill already has 6 points and making clubs trumps will cost her 1 point for gift and thus the entire game. Mary must run the cards. Accordingly she deals three more to Bill and then three to herself.

The hands become:

Mary   **Bill**

♠J ◇K Q 4 3 ♣A 7 ♡J 4   ♠A Q ◇A 8 7 5 ♣Q ♡10 8

Turn-up: ♡7

The new turn-up is different from the original one, so hearts are trumps, and neither player has any choice in the matter. They both discard three cards to give these hands:

Mary   **Bill**

♠J ◇K Q ♣A ♡J 4   ♠A Q ◇A ♣Q ♡10 8

The play is as follows:

Mary	Bill (to lead)
	♠ Q
♡ 4	
(Mary's trick)	
◇ Q	
	◇ A
	(Bill's trick)
	♣ Q
♣ A	
(Mary's trick)	
♠ J	
	♡ 8
	(Bill's trick)
	♠ A
♡ J	
(Mary's trick)	
◇ K	
	♡ 10
	(Bill's trick)

Mary has scored 1 for high (jack of hearts), 1 for low (four of hearts), both of which she was dealt, and 1 for the jack of hearts she has captured in play, a total of 3 from the hand. As for game, Mary counts 8 (two aces), 4 (two queens) and 1 (one jack), that is 13 high-card points in all. Bill has one ten for 10, an ace for 4, and 3 for a king, 2 for a queen and 1 for a jack. He has scored 20 high-card points.

20–13 gives Bill 1 for game but in the event this is academic. Mary began the hand with 4 and since the cards are counted in the order high, low, jack, game, the 3 she has scored give her the necessary 7 to win before Bill can count his 1.

HINTS ON PLAY

Every deal in Seven Up turns on what becomes trumps. In deciding to accept or reject the trump turn-up, a player needs to estimate whether he holds a card likely to be the highest trump and one likely to be the lowest, whether he has sufficient high-card strength to capture the jack if it is in play, and whether he has the length in trumps which will nearly always enable him to capture the scoring cards necessary to win the game point. In a game where some of the cards remain undealt in the pack there can be no means of arriving at a precise mathematical assessment, but in general the chances for any high card except the ace, and for any low card except the two, diminish as both the number of players in the deal and the number of cards run increase. The best holding is a minimum of three trumps including at least one court card and one 'rag'. Even an ace or a king, and one low card, have sound prospects; for two trumps will often be sufficient to draw the opposition trumps and set up high cards in side suits.

It is vital to play to the score. So needing only 1 point for seven up, a lone ace in trumps will certainly secure a win, and even a singleton king should be enough to get the point for high which is always counted first. Only a complete novice would reject these cards and try for a new suit as trumps in which he has greater length. Again, in such a position, a solitary two or three is acceptable for trumps, provided an opponent does not also want just 1 point for game which he will score high before low for any better trump.

Beyond that, everything in Seven Up is pretty much a guess. In the play of the tricks, since there is no requirement to follow suit and an opponent may use a trump to capture a high card led to him, no cards except the very top trumps are safe. Tens sometimes play a big part in determining the fate of the game point. By careful play, a ten in hand guarded by at least one other card can often be won back in a trick.

So Seven Up contains a lot of guesswork and few certainties. It is the fashion nowadays to evaluate the respective merits of card games by the degree of skill they involve. On the other hand a great deal of pleasure can be derived from games where luck plays a significant part. If Seven Up is definitely in the latter category, this does not mean that is is not a good game. It has many interesting features and in its original form is at least four hundred years old. It has stood the test of time, and that is a recommendation in itself.

AUCTION PITCH

Nowadays the most popular 'All Fours' game in the United States is Auction Pitch, which is a version of Seven Up with a round of bidding. It is also known as Setback, or simply as Pitch because the highest bidder 'pitches' a card to fix the trump suit.

HOW TO PLAY

Any number from two to seven may play, but it is generally agreed that four make the best game. There are no partnerships.

As in the parent game of Seven Up, the cards rank in the Whist order from ace (high) to two (low). Players cut for deal in the normal way and the right to deal, like bidding and play, moves round the table to the left. Six cards are dealt to each player in two batches of three. However, no card is turned up from the pack to propose the trump suit.

Four points (for high, low, jack, game) are available to be won in a deal. Beginning with the player at the left of the dealer, each has one chance to bid or pass. There are four bids: one, two, three or four. No suit is mentioned by any player making a bid. A player may indicate that he bids four by pitching, that is by making an opening lead. This immediately terminates the auction. If all pass, the cards are redealt by the same dealer.

The player who has made the highest bid becomes the 'pitcher' for the round and plays a card. Its suit determines trumps for the deal. Although the highest bidder is not required to name a trump suit before pitching, if he does so but leads a different suit, it is the lead card which makes trumps.

The rules for the play of the tricks are as in Seven Up. To a trump led at any stage, all the other players must play a trump if they have one. Otherwise they can discard from some other suit. A hand which is able to follow in a side suit may either do so or trump. So a trump may be played even when a player can follow suit. If a player cannot follow and holds no trump, then he discards from a third suit. There is no requirement for a player to try to win a trick should he choose not to. A trick is won by the highest trump it contains, or if it contains no trump, by the highest card played of the suit led. The winner of a trick leads to the next.

The four points to be won in play are the same as in Seven Up; namely 1 point for the highest trump in play and 1 point for the lowest (scored by the players to whom they were originally dealt), 1 point for winning the jack of trumps in a trick if it is in play, and 1 point for game. The game point goes to the player who at the end of the deal has won in his tricks the highest total for valuable cards, counting 10 for each ten, 4 for an ace, 3 for a king, 2 for a queen and 1 for a jack. If there is a tie for game, no one scores the point.

Where there is only a single trump in play, it scores 2 points for both high and low. Should it be a jack, the additional point goes to the player who captures it in a trick.

When the six tricks have been played, the pitcher scores for all he has made, provided he has made at least as many points as he bid. So if he bids 'two' and makes 3, he scores 3. If however he wins less points than he bid, he is 'set back' and the full value of his bid is deducted from his overall score. So a pitcher bidding 'two' and making only 1 point, loses 2 points. Thus minus scores are possible in Auction Pitch and a player with a minus total is said to be 'in the hole', denoted by drawing a circle around his score. Irrespective of how the pitcher fares on a deal, each opponent scores individually what he himself has made from the four possible points.

The first player to reach 7 points from a series of deals wins the game. If the pitcher and one or more of the other players reach 7 points on the same deal, the pitcher wins. As between the other players, the points are counted in the strict order, high, low, jack, game, to determine an outright winner.

The game is traditionally 'seven up' but in some schools 9, 10, 11 or even 21, rather than 7, constitute a completed game by agreement among all the players.

The rules for a revoke in Auction Pitch differ from those in Seven Up to take into account the fact that the former is a bidding game. As in the original game, a revoke is defined as either failing to play a trump to a trump lead when a player holds a trump, or discarding from a third suit when he can in fact follow to the lead in a side suit or is able to trump.

At Auction Pitch however, a revoke may not be corrected. So a card played is irrevocably played and may not be taken back, even if the next player has yet to play a card to the trick. After the six tricks have been completed, the penalty for the revoke is imposed.

If the pitcher revoked, he scores nothing for any of the points he has made but is set back the full amount of his bid which is deducted from his total score. Each of the other players score the points they themselves have made as individuals. Should a player other than the pitcher revoke, he too receives no credit for any points he may have made, and the value of the prevailing bid is deducted from his running total. The others score what points they have made, including the pitcher regardless of whether or not he actually succeeded in his bid.

THE PLAY OF A HAND

Here is a deal between Mary, Bill, Jane and Paul which fully illustrates the bidding and play at Auction Pitch.

Mary (dealer): ♠Q 5 ◇2 ♣A Q ♡4

Bill: ♠A 7 2 ◇— ♣6 5 ♡J

Jane: ♠K 3 ◇3 ♣8 ♡5 3

Paul: ♠— ◇A Q ♣K 2 ♡Q 7

Bill is first to bid. With spades as trumps, he has the ace and two, so he is certain of the high and low points. He has a cast-iron bid of 'two', but will his three trumps be good enough to win the game point for him and justify a call of 'three'? He has only a bare jack outside the spades and as first to bid it usually pays to be cautious. He calls 'two'.

Jane has a poor hand. She has a possible high and low in spades but little prospect of scoring for anything else. Clearly she cannot bid over Bill's 'two' and so she passes.

Paul on the other hand has good cards. If he makes clubs trumps, he will win the low point with the two and might well score for high with the king. Provided there are not three clubs against him in one hand, his outside strength could give him the game point. He risks a bid of 'three'.

Mary has no hope of getting anything like the four needed to outbid Paul. She passes.

Paul is the pitcher with his bid of three and makes the opening lead. This is the king of clubs and so clubs are trumps.

The diagram on the following page shows how the game then developed.

Mary	Bill	Jane	Paul
			♣K
♣A			
	♣5		
		♣8	
(Mary's trick)			
♠5			
	♣6		
		♠3	
			♣2
	(Bill's trick)		
	♠2		
		♠K	
			♡7
♠Q			
		(Jane's trick)	
		♡3	
			♡Q
♡4			
	♡J		
			(Paul's trick)
			◇Q
◇2			
	♠7		
		◇3	
			(Paul's trick)
			◇A
♣Q			
	♠A		
		♡5	
(Mary's trick)			

Paul's calculations have gone badly wrong. He scores 1 point for low (two of clubs), but Mary's ace of clubs turned out to be the highest trump, for which she counts 1. The jack of trumps was not in play, so no one scores for it. In the tricks Mary has captured three aces, a king and a queen, for 17 against Paul's two queens and a jack for only 5. Jane also has 5, from a king and a queen, and Bill's single trick had no high cards at all. Mary has won the game point.

Paul bid, 'three' but made only 1 point. Since this was the first deal of the game there were no scores on the sheet and he goes 3 in the hole. Mary receives 2 for high and game. Jane and Bill fail to score. Paul has made a poor beginning in his quest for 7 points to win the overall game through what turned out to be a rash bid. Mary by contrast has got off to a flying start.

HINTS ON PLAY

Most of the skill at Auction Pitch is exercised in the bidding. Although no suits are mentioned, the dealer hears the other players' assessments of their hands. He has a slight advantage in bidding last and should take the most optimistic view of his prospects. It generally pays him to take a chance or two in order to win the call. Players who must bid earlier in the deal, on the other hand, should err on the side of caution.

Length is important for a potential trump suit, and three trumps will often win the point for game. However, three intermediate cards are not particularly good because they are unlikely to score for high or low. Tens and aces in side suits enhance the prospects of a hand for game point, but since an opponent may trump even if he can follow suit, they may easily be lost in play and cannot be relied upon for bidding purposes.

In the play of the tricks the pitcher nearly always does best by drawing trumps straightaway in the hope of clearing the way for his high cards in side suits. All the opponents should whenever possible throw away any tens to a fellow defender who seems likely to win a trick. This sacrifice reduces the pitcher's chances of making the game point.

SMUDGE

Smudge is a major variant of the game. It is played in the same way as Auction Pitch but with two important points of difference:

i) High, jack and game are scored for as in Pitch, but low is counted by the player who wins the lowest trump in play in a trick, regardless of to whom it was originally dealt. If there is only one trump out, which is very unlikely, the point for high is won by the player to whom it was dealt while the low point goes to whoever captures it in a trick. If it happens to be a jack, the additional point is won by the player who takes it in a trick.

ii) Smudge is a bid of four. If a player goes smudge and makes all four points, he wins the game in one deal. However, if he was in the hole his successful smudge bid merely reduces his deficit by 4. A failed smudge counts 4 against its bidder and the other players score what they have made as individuals.

Although a successful bid of four wins an instant victory from even a zero score, 7 points are needed to make a completed game from lesser bids and scores. Variants where game is 9, 10, 11 or 21 are not permitted.

Auction Pitch is by no stretch of the imagination a leading card game. As in its forerunner Seven Up, a large element of luck is involved on every deal. However it is a good, fast gambling game and this no doubt accounts for its continued popularity across the Atlantic.

EIGHTS

Also known in America as Crazy Eights and Swedish Rummy, Eights is the most popular modern version of an eighteenth century English game called Comet in celebration of the celestial body predicted by Edmund Halley. Although two players make the most skilful game, Eights can be played by up to seven and is just the thing for a family gathering where children can play with adults in an enjoyable game that is not too demanding.

HOW TO PLAY

When two play, each receives seven cards from the regular fifty-two card pack. Three to five players begin with only five cards from the same standard deck, but with six or seven in the game, two full packs are shuffled together and the players are dealt five cards each.

The object of the game is straightforward. By playing at their turn a card of the same suit or the same rank as the previous card put down by an opponent, the players try to get rid of all their cards. The first to succeed in doing this wins the deal and receives points from the others in accordance with the penalty value of the cards left in their hands.

Players cut for deal. Ace ranks low and whoever cuts the lowest card becomes dealer. Thereafter the right to deal moves round the table to the left.

The dealer serves out to each player the required number of cards depending on how many participate. He begins with the player on his immediate left and moving round the table in a clockwise direction, distributes the cards one at a time. The deal is completed by turning up the top card from the undealt pack. This is known as the 'starter'. The remainder of the pack is placed face down next to the starter to form the 'stock' from which the players will draw during play.

The first turn belongs to the player to the left of the dealer and the turn to play moves round the table in the same direction as the deal. A turn consists of placing a single card face up on a pile begun by the starter. Each card played must match the preceding one in either suit or rank. So for example on the nine of diamonds, any diamond or a nine of some other suit can be played. If a diamond is played, the next player has the same option of matching it with a further diamond or a card of the same rank. If another nine is played, this changes the suit and the player who is next to go must follow to the new suit or put down yet another nine, and so on.

A short sequence of cards in the play of a four-handed deal will make the basic procedure absolutely clear, although in an actual game each card is placed face up on the previous card played in a single pile.

first player	second player	third player	fourth player
◇9	◇Q	♣Q	♣4
♠6	♠A	♠3	♣3
♣10	♣5	♣J	♣Q

If a player cannot play a card when it is his turn, he must draw from the unexposed stock until he is able to do so. Players may also draw as many cards as they wish from the stock even though they hold a card in hand that is in fact playable. Irrespective of how many cards are drawn, each turn must be completed by the play of a card to the pile of turned up cards. The only time a player may pass is when he has no playable card in his hand and the stock has been completely exhausted. In this event he misses his turn and only plays again, if he can do so, when his next turn comes round.

Eights are 'wild' cards, that is they may be played on any preceding card regardless of its suit or rank. The player of an eight must specify the suit he requires subsequent players to match, which may be its own or a different one. The player whose turn comes next must then either play a card of the suit nominated or put down another eight. In the latter case he too would specify the next suit to be played to. This makes eights the most powerful cards in the pack, for whenever a player puts down an eight he is able to shift the whole course of the game in the direction which is most to his liking. He may of course use the wild card to stipulate that the suit already being played should be continued.

A problem occurs when an eight is dealt as the starter card. The usual solution is to put the eight back into the stock which is then thoroughly shuffled before a new card is turned up as the starter.

Play ceases when any player manages to get rid of the final card in his hand onto the pile of exposed cards. He collects as a reward the penalty value of the cards left in each of the losing hands according to the following scale:

Each eight	50
Each king, queen, jack	10
Each ace	1
Any other card	face value

In games involving several players, it is usual to settle each deal as a separate game. When two play however, the normal practice is to award the game to whoever first scores 100 points from a series of successive deals.

Sometimes a deal ends in a 'block', that is no hand is able to play and all the stock cards have been transferred to the exposed pile which may not of course be drawn from. In this event the players total the penalty points for the cards they have left in their hands. The player with the lowest total wins the deal and collects from each of the others the difference between his winning and their losing count. If there is a tie, the winners divide the points from the losing hands between them.

THE PLAY OF A HAND

Here is a full deal between Jane and Bill which illustrates all the fundamental principles of play at Eights.

Bill (dealer)   **Jane**

♣4 A ♡10 9 ◇10 9 ♣6   ♠8 3 ♡J ◇Q 4 ♣Q 7

              ◇2 (starter)
              ◇Q (Jane)
              ◇9 (Bill)
              ◇4 (Jane)
              ◇10 (Bill)

                                              Jane has no diamonds and no ten. She does have an eight but does not wish to play it so early. She draws two cards, picking up the ten of clubs last, to hold:

                                              ♠8 3 ♡J ◇— ♣Q 10 7 4

              ♣10 (Jane)
              ♡10 (Bill)
              ♡J (Jane)
              ♡9 (Bill)

♣8 (Jane)

> Jane has played her wild card. She specifies clubs as the new suit.

♣6 (Bill)

♣Q (Jane)

Bill is now unable to go. He draws two cards, then the king of clubs and holds:
♠4 A ♡K ◇7 ♣K

♣K (Bill)

♣7 (Jane)

◇7 (Bill)

> Jane cannot play. She draws one card and now has:
>
> ♠3 ◇A ♣4

◇A (Jane)

♠A (Bill)

♠3 (Jane)

♠4 (Bill)

♣4 (Jane)

So Jane has got rid of all her cards and wins the deal. Bill is left with the king of hearts which has a penalty value of 10 points. This is credited to Jane's score.

HINTS ON PLAY

It is obvious from the above deal that a great deal of luck enters into Eights. On the other hand it is possible by employing certain basic tactics for a player to increase his chances of winning. These tactics are best suited to the two-handed game where technically correct play is most likely to succeed. However, since the advice set out below is based on sound principles, it also applies to some extent to games with a lot of players.

Ideally, as the game proceeds, a player should try to remember all the cards played so far. This will enable him on occasion to make a correct decision in play which would otherwise be a pure guess. This is very much a counsel of perfection. Eights is played fairly rapidly and such a feat of memory is not within everyone's compass. If a player remembers nothing else however, he should at least know how many eights have been played.

They are the key cards in the game and often exercise a vital influence on the most important stages of the deal.

The basic strategy of Eights is to play from long suits and to keep on doing so at every opportunity. This gives a player the best prospect of reducing his own hand, and since he is long in a suit it may well be that the opposition will be short in it and so be forced to draw cards from the stock.

Once an opponent indicates by his play that he has no cards in a suit, it should be played against him whenever possible. Whatever he does to combat this tactic, the odds are that he will have to take extra cards from the stock each time the suit is played. So eights are at their most powerful when used to switch back to an opponent's weak suit. Also, in maintaining pressure of this kind, if a player has a choice he should play cards of which he has others of the same rank in his hand. So with hearts being played and the opponent known to be weak in them, a player who has say three hearts including the ten, and two other tens in his hand, should put down the ten of hearts. The opponent will be extremely lucky to hold the other ten that will enable him to switch the game away from his vulnerable suit. Again he may have to pick up a large number of cards before he draws one to relieve the pressure.

Normally it is poor play to use an eight early in the deal merely to avoid drawing from the stock. An eight or eights should be saved for later when they are most effective as a means of exploiting any weakness in the opposition's hand. Equally eights may be used to rescue their holder from a tight corner into which he himself may have been driven at a vital stage of the game.

Drawing cards from the stock when it is unnecessary to do so is always a gamble. It is sometimes done early on in the hope of picking up an eight or of strengthening a long suit which could be used to put pressure on an opponent. However, there is no guarantee that the required cards are near the top of the pack and the tactic is just as likely to fail as to succeed, sometimes with disastrous consequences. By and large it is best to draw cards only when forced to do so.

Eights is a fun game in which luck often plays the decisive part, however adroitly a player manages his cards. Yet it has some excellent features which add up to splendid entertainment. It is ideal for those times when like-minded people wish to have a good game of cards without getting too serious about it.

MICHIGAN

Also called Saratoga, Michigan is the American equivalent of the English game of Newmarket. It is the most popular of the 'stops' family of games in which the sequence of cards being played is 'stopped' by a missing card. Though the players make bets on certain cards, stakes either in the form of chips or small coins are invariably kept to the very minimum in what is essentially a party game for all ages.

HOW TO PLAY

Any number from three to eight can play. The standard pack of fifty-two cards is used and the sequence of cards in each of the four suits is two (low), three, four, five, six, seven, eight, nine, ten, jack, queen, king, ace (high). In addition four cards are taken from a second deck and placed face up on the table in a square. These form the 'layout' and are called the 'boodle' cards. They are:

> Ace of hearts
> King of clubs
> Queen of diamonds
> Jack of spades

The right to deal is decided by any player picking up the full pack, shuffling it thoroughly and giving one card at a time to each player until a jack is exposed. Its recipient becomes the dealer for the first hand. Thereafter the deal rotates round the table to the left and the game is completed when all the participants have dealt a round of cards.

Before the deal the players must all place chips on the boodle cards in the table layout from the equal number given to each at the start of the game. The dealer must put two chips on each of the four cards, while the others are required to stake only a single chip per boodle card.

There are two objectives in Michigan. If a player has a card in his hand which matches a boodle card, he tries to play it and so collect all the chips placed on that card in the layout. Also the first player to get rid of the whole of his hand receives chips from the others according to how many cards they have left unplayed in their hands.

Beginning with the player at his immediate left, the first dealer serves out the cards singly to each player including himself in a clockwise direction. He also gives cards to an extra hand known as the 'widow'. He goes on dealing in this manner until every card in the pack has been distributed. This means that in all but a three-handed game some players will receive one more card than the others. Since each player will eventually deal once in a full game however, this slight discrepancy is cancelled out over a complete rota of deals.

The deal completed, the players examine their hands, but before actual play begins the fate of the widow has to be settled. If the dealer wishes, he can exchange the hand he has been dealt for the spare hand without further payment. He does not look at the widow before exercising this option and if he does decide on an exchange, he cannot take back the original hand which he has just discarded face down without showing it to the rest of the players. Should he not want to swap his hand for the widow, it is the dealer's duty to auction it among the players. Whoever bids the highest number of chips for the extra hand becomes its owner. Having once purchased the widow and looked at it, the successful bidder may not revert to the hand he was initially dealt. This he discards unexposed on the table and pays the value of his bid to the dealer.

Play is started by the player to the left of the dealer. He puts down one card from any suit of his choice but it must be the lowest card in his hand of that suit. If he is able to follow with the next highest card in the suit, he does so and goes on playing until he is 'stopped' and can no longer continue the sequence. Then the player who does hold the next card must lay it down. Thus the turn to play does not go in strict rotation round the table as in most card games, but passes to whoever is able to carry on the sequence of cards in progress.

It is usual for the players to announce the card they are playing as they put it out face up on the table, saying 'four of spades', 'five of spades', 'six of spades', and so on. As the game proceeds, they keep the cards they have played in front of them in separate piles, so that only the last card is showing, and they are not permitted to look through them to discover what cards have already gone.

A sequence is eventually stopped because it reaches the ace of the suit or because the next card is unavailable. It may be in the dead extra hand or, later in the game, it could be contained in some previously played sequence. The player who puts down the last card in a sequence which cannot be continued is then entitled to play a card of his choice. However, he must change the suit and he must play the lowest card he has in the new suit, announcing the denomination and the suit in the normal way. If he finds himself unable to change the suit, he must pass and the turn to play moves to his left. Should no player be able to begin a new suit, the turn reverts to the player who originally passed. He then puts out the lowest card of those remaining in his hand.

When in the course of play someone is able to lay down from his hand a card which matches one of the four boodle cards, he collects the whole of the stakes placed on it.

The deal ends as soon as one player gets rid of the final card in his hand. He collects from each of the other players one chip for each card left in their respective hands. If none of the players can play off all their cards, the player who is left with the fewest cards is the winner. When two or more players have an equal number of unplayable cards, the stakes from the losing players are shared between them.

It sometimes happens that not all the boodle cards are matched during a deal. In that event the uncollected chips remain in place on the relevant cards in the layout to boost the normal stakes to be won on the following hand.

After all the players have dealt a round of cards and the game is thereby completed, the one who has amassed the greatest number of chips is the overall winner.

THE PLAY OF A HAND

Here is a deal with Mary, Bill and Jane. Mary is the dealer and stakes eight chips equally between the four boodle cards. Bill and Jane place only one chip on each, so that every card in the layout is worth four chips.

The hands are:

Mary (dealer): ♡Q 4 3 ♣8 4 ♢A Q 10 5 ♠J 9 5 2

Bill: ♡9 2 ♣A K Q 10 9 6 5 ♢3 ♠A Q 8

Jane: ♡J 10 7 6 5 ♣7 2 ♢K J 7 ♠6 4 3

Widow (unexposed)

Mary as dealer looks at her hand. She has two boodle cards, the queen of diamonds and the jack of spades, as well as a fair sprinkling of high cards which should come in useful in the closing stages of the deal. There is absolutely no point in exchanging such a good hand for the unknown widow which is very unlikely to be any better. She does not hesitate to offer the spare hand for auction in the hope of collecting some chips for it.

Bill has an interesting hand. He holds the boodle king of clubs and a long club suit. In two of the other suits however, he lacks high cards. He decides to pin his faith on the clubs. If he can gain the lead enough times to run that suit, he might collect on the king and could emerge as the winner with either clubs or spades being played at the end of the hand. He decides not to bid for the widow.

Jane has picked up some poor cards. To begin with, there is no boodle card. She has some high cards which might eventually win the hand for her, but she also has quite a few low ones that could be difficult to get rid of. Jane opens the auction by bidding one chip for the widow.

Bill has already passed, but he may still make a bid if he wishes. However, he decides to stick to his original plan and passes again. Jane has got the widow cheaply and pays the dealer, Mary, a single chip for it, discarding the hand she was dealt face down on the table.

The hands are now:

Mary (dealer): ♡Q 4 3 ♣8 4 ♢A Q 10 5 ♠J 9 5 2

Bill: ♡9 2 ♣A K Q 10 9 6 5 ♢3 ♠A Q 8

Jane: ♡A K 8 ♣J 3 ♢9 8 6 4 2 ♠K 10 7

The play goes as follows:

Mary	Bill	Jane
	♣5	
	♣6	
	(♣7 in dead hand)	
	◇3	
		◇4
◇5		
		◇6
		(◇7 in dead hand)
		♡8
	♡9	
	(♡10 in dead hand)	
	♣9	
	♣10	
		♣J
	♣Q	
	♣K (collects 4 chips)	
	♣A	
	♡2	
♡3		
♡4		
(♡5 in dead hand)		
♣4		
(♣5 already played)		
♠2		
(♠3 in dead hand)		
◇10		
(◇J in dead hand)		
♣8		

Mary	Bill	Jane
(♣9 already played)		
◇Q (collects 4 chips)		
◇K (in dead hand)		
♠5		
(♠6 in dead hand)		
◇A		
♠9		
		♠10
♠J (collects 4 chips)		
	♠Q	
		♠K
	♠A	
	(Bill cannot change suit. Turn passes to Jane)	
		♡K
		♡A (collects 4 chips)
		♣3
		(♣4 already played)
		◇2
		(◇3 already played)
		♠7
	♠8 (last card)	
(left with ♡Q)		(left with ◇98)

Bill's decision to rely on one long suit and hope for the best has worked out very well. He receives one chip from Mary and two from Jane for winning the deal. He also gained four chips from the boodle king of clubs, so he has pulled in a total of seven chips during the round. Since he staked four on the layout, he comes out with an overall gain of three chips.

Mary has collected eight chips from boodle cards plus one from the auction, but because she was not the first to get rid of all her cards she has to pay one chip back to Bill. She has thus gained eight chips in all during the round. However, as dealer she had to lay out eight chips, so she has only broken even on the deal.

Jane got four chips from the boodle ace of hearts, less the two chips she has to pay Bill for the cards left in her hand, less another chip paid for the widow, making a gain of one chip overall during play. She originally staked four chips on the layout which means that she ends the deal by losing a total of three chips.

HINTS ON PLAY

Michigan is so simple to learn and play that it is easy to lose sight of the fact that the game definitely offers opportunities for skilled play and that poor technique will prove costly in the long run.

The first problem that confronts players is whether or not to bid for the widow. Here the dealer is in a much easier position than his rivals. Almost any reasonable hand, that is one that contains at least one boodle card and a good number of high cards is preferable to the widow which may have nothing worth having at all. Dealt a worse hand than this, the dealer has no problem. He takes the widow, for it costs him nothing. The choice is harder for his opponents when they pick up a hand with few high ranking cards and no matches in the layout however. By and large they should be wary of paying even a few chips for the spare hand. There is no guarantee of thereby gaining a better holding and the mathematics of Michigan are such that the widow needs to be really good to recover the cost of its purchase in a brisk auction. Bidding too freely for the widow is a common fault among inexperienced players. More often than not, dealt a bad hand, it pays to sit and suffer unless the widow can be obtained very cheaply. It is very much a matter of temperament. The gambler may think the risk of an expensive widow worthwhile, but it will be the cautious players who reap the benefit in the long run, for in Michigan, as in most card games, it is they who usually come out on top.

In the play the beginner invariably starts by leading a suit in which he has a boodle card and goes on playing this suit at every opportunity. This is not necessarily the correct play. There is always a good chance of winning chips from layout cards without forcing the issue, since the other players will play off their high cards in an attempt to get rid of the whole of their hand. It is often much better to make a positive try for the game right from the beginning. The proper way to do this is to reduce a hand's longest suit whenever possible. This offers the best chance of getting rid of a lot of cards quickly and so creating a winning position. If the long suit contains a boodle card, well and good; if not, the odds are that a boodle will be developed naturally as the result of competitive play near the end of the deal.

It is essential in play to try to remember the cards which are used to start each new sequence. So if someone begins a sequence with the seven of clubs for example, a player can safely play off the six of the suit later on, knowing that the sequence must immediately be stopped. The lead is thereby retained and a card has been got rid of at no cost which, if kept, might prove extremely troublesome in subsequent play. If more than one card below such a stop is held, the suit should still be played. So holding the two as well as the six in this example, the two is played. The sequence could easily run to the six via the other players, and even if it fails to do so, there will be the opportunity to get rid of the six when the lead is regained.

There is one further point for the really skilful player. Anyone who exchanges his original hand for the widow automatically knows all the natural stops in the game because he knows the contents of the discarded hand. This may provide vital information in deciding the best card to play at a crucial stage of the game. However, quite apart from the feat of memory involved, it takes a really clever player to capitalise on this advantage, and it must be said that in what is really a party game, such refined calculations may not be appreciated by others in the company.

So Michigan is a social game, and one of the very best of its kind. Its combination of luck and skill, spiced by the element of gambling involved, provides plenty of interest and amusement which invariably makes for an exciting contest. It is not difficult to understand why it is a favourite with all sorts of American families.

RED DOG

Red Dog is a gambling game much played by American servicemen. It is also very popular among journalists for moments of relaxation when the scent of the news trail has temporarily grown cold. Such games are often for high stakes, but Red Dog makes an excellent party game too. For instance the late Duchess of Windsor records in her memoirs that it was Red Dog which provided the evening entertainment during a country house party on the occasion of one of her first meetings with the then Prince of Wales at the beginning of their historic relationship. In fact it is just the game to play when any group of family or friends come together at a social gathering. It also known as High-Card Pool in the United States.

The mechanics of Red Dog are extremely simple but the game calls for considerable mental agility, for the chances of success on an individual bet can be calculated very precisely.

HOW TO PLAY

Any number from two to ten can play, but the game is rather dull two-handed and a medium number ensures the right combination of interest and skill.

The standard fifty-two card pack is used and the cards rank in their most natural order, namely ace (high), king, queen, jack, ten, nine, eight, seven, six, five, four, three, two (low). Except in very heavy gambling games where ready cash is wagered, chips are distributed among the players before play begins.

Any player picks up the deck and after shuffling it, deals one card to each participant in rotation. The first to receive an ace becomes the dealer for the opening round. Thereafter the deal moves round the table to the left. Each player is dealt four cards one at a time in a clockwise direction starting with the player at the dealer's left. The remainder of the pack is placed face down in front of the dealer.

Before they look at their cards all the players, including the dealer, 'ante' one chip (or more by agreement) into the pool. The object of the game is for each player to try to beat the top card of the undealt pack by holding a higher ranking card of the same suit in his hand. At their turn the players bet against the pool on whether they can do so.

The player to the left of the dealer goes first. A player may stake from one chip up to the total number of chips in the pool at the time he makes his bet. If he places such a maximum bet, he is said to 'bet the pot'. Once he has specified the amount of his stake and put the required number of chips before him on the table, the dealer turns up the top card of the pack. Should the player who has bet be able to produce a higher card of the same suit from his hand, he takes back his chips plus an equal number from the pool. He then discards the remainder of his hand on the table without showing the cards to the other players. If however he cannot beat the card turned up by the dealer, his losing stake is added to the pool and the whole of his hand is exposed before finally being discarded face down, after which it may not be looked at again by the subsequent players.

The turn to bet moves clockwise round the table until all the players have made a bet, and either won or lost. The dealer concludes the betting for the deal. The cards are then gathered in, shuffled and the next player becomes the new dealer when the same cycle of betting is repeated on a fresh round of cards with a new ante of one chip per player.

If at any time during play the pot is reduced to zero, each player antes again as at the start of a deal and the game goes on in the normal way. Since the maximum stake allowed is the size of the pot, the pool is always able to meet its obligations on a bet.

THE PLAY OF A HAND

The art of Red Dog lies in counting the cards in such a way as to calculate whether the chance of winning is greater than the chance of losing. A deal involving Jane, Paul and Mary will demonstrate the play and how this assessment is made.

Jane is the dealer and after each of the three have anted one chip into the pool, Paul who is at her left looks at his four cards. They are:

♠Q ♡J ♢Q J

Paul calculates that there are two spades (ace and king), three hearts (ace, king, queen), two diamonds (ace and king) and all thirteen clubs which he will be unable to beat, a total of twenty cards. Since there are forty-eight cards he cannot see, this means that there must be twenty-eight which he can better. The odds are therefore 28 to 20, or 7 or 5, on that he will win. This is a better than even chance and Paul decides to bet two chips against the pot. Jane as dealer turns up the top card from the pack. It is the ace of hearts, which is unbeatable. The best Paul can do is the jack of the suit. Despite the original odds being in his favour, he has lost. He pays his two chips to the pool which is thereby increased to five chips. Paul also shows the whole of his losing hand to the rest of the players before throwing it away face down.

Mary goes next. Her hand is:

♣K J ♣A 4

She does her mental arithmetic. She has no hearts and no diamonds but she has seen two cards of each suit exposed on Paul's turn. Therefore there are twenty-two cards (twenty-six less four) left in the red suits which she will be unable to beat. She holds the ace of clubs and the king of spades, so only one card, the ace of spades, is against her in the black suits. This means there are twenty-three cards in all to which she can lose. Of the original fifty-two cards in the pack the whereabouts of nine, including the four in her hand, are known to her. So from the remaining forty-three cards, she will lose to twenty-three and must be able to better twenty. This is only slightly worse than an even chance. Mary risks a bet of two chips.

The top card of the pack turns out to be the five of clubs. Mary has won. She shows her ace of clubs and collects two chips from the pool which is now reduced to three chips. The rest of her hand she puts face down on the table without showing it to the others.

Jane, the dealer, plays last. She holds:

◇8 7 ♣6 2

This is a poor hand. Jane has no hearts and since only two hearts have already been exposed, there are eleven cards against her in this suit. She also has no spades. Thirteen less the queen of spades which she knows is out of the pack leaves twelve spades that will beat her. There are six cards in diamonds above her eight, but Paul has already exposed two of them, so she could lose to one of four diamonds. Similarly there are eight cards higher than her six of clubs, but the ace has already been shown by Mary, leaving seven against her in clubs. Eleven hearts, twelve spades, four diamonds and seven clubs add up to a total thirty-four cards to which she will lose. Five cards were revealed on Paul's turn, two on Mary's, and Jane can see four in her own hand. So there are fifty-two less five, less two, less four, that is forty-one cards which she must contend with. Since thirty-four cards are against her, there can only be seven for, making odds of nearly 5–1 against. However, she must bet at least one chip. This she does and to her grateful surprise turns up the four of diamonds. Jane has won against the odds, for she can produce a higher diamond from her hand. She wins one chip.

After this round there remain two chips in the pot to boost the ante of one chip due from each player on the next round when Paul will be the dealer.

HINTS ON PLAY

Red Dog is usually played at a fast and furious pace, so exact calculations of odds and chances as outlined above obviously call for formidable arithmetical powers, and the task becomes more difficult the later in a round a player's turn comes and the greater the number of players in the game. In fact ordinary mortals make only a rough appraisal of the odds and bet accordingly. In any case, as with Jane's hand in the sample deal, the turn of the cards can make nonsense of mathematical probabilities.

Nevertheless, the later players in a round have a definite advantage. They have seen more cards than those who have gone earlier and can sometimes find themselves in a position where they are almost certain to succeed and can bet confidently with a very high stake. So the dealer, who always goes last, is the most favoured of all. However, it is an important feature of Red Dog that the right to deal passes from player to player. So the disadvantage of betting nearer the beginning of a round than the end is completely cancelled out over a full rota of deals.

Sometimes in friendly games five cards are dealt to each player. This makes the job of estimating the mathematical chance of success even more complex and has the effect of giving everyone a more equal chance against the would-be expert who is bent on counting every card and relies on mathematics to give him the edge. If however nine or ten play, only four cards may be dealt to each player. Otherwise there will not be enough cards in the deck to complete a full cycle of bets.

Despite its somewhat evil reputation as a gambling game which attracts big money, Red Dog can also be enjoyed in a party spirit. It is an action game that is fun to play in good company and provides an excellent challenge for the serious and not-so-serious card player alike.

RUSSIAN BANK

An old French game called *Crapette* was the forerunner of modern Russian Bank which is a favourite pastime in the United States. It is really a double solitaire where the players each begin with a full pack of fifty-two cards and try to be the first to get rid of them all. They can do this in a variety of ways with foundations built up in suit and sequence on the eight aces at the centre of the game. Because it contains the element of competition, Russian Bank is much more interesting than the usual sorts of patience.

HOW TO PLAY

The two regular fifty-two card decks should have different backs so that they can be easily sorted after the completion of each game. The sequence of the cards is natural: ace, two, three, four, five, six, seven, eight, nine, ten, jack, queen, king.

Before the game begins each player fans out his deck face down on the table and selects one card. Whoever draws the lower card has the first turn. Each then shuffles his pack thoroughly and has it cut by his opponent.

To form the layout both players deal out twelve cards face down and place them on the table in a pile at their right. These cards constitute each player's 'stock'. Next the top card of each stock is exposed. Then the players each deal four cards face up in a line away from their stocks and towards the opponent. These lines of cards together make up the 'tableau' and are placed so as to allow two extra lines between them that will eventually accomodate the 'centre piles' on which suits are built in their natural order from the aces upwards. Finally both players put the undealt remainder of their respective packs directly in front of them face down to form their 'hands'. Once play is in progress there will be a waste pile for each player which goes to the left of the hand.

Here is the full layout for Russian Bank before the player who is to start has had his first turn:

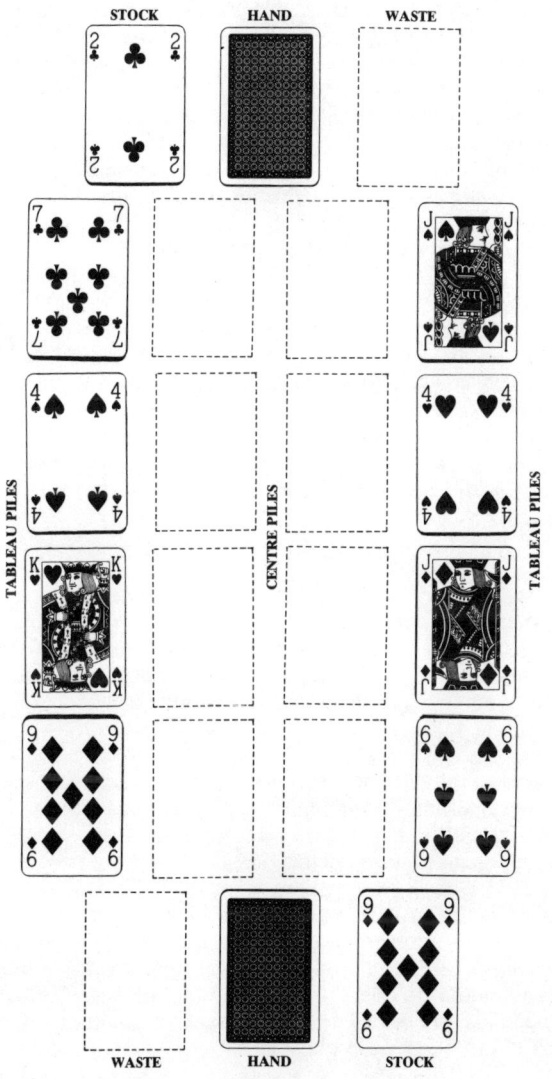

The game is most easily understood if its various aspects are considered under a series of separate headings as follows.
Order of precedence

i) Any exposed card which can be transferred into a centre pile, whether from the top of a player's stock, from the top of a tableau pile, or from hand, must be placed there in preference to any other play. The first card to go into any centre pile will be an ace, followed by cards of the same suit in ascending natural order, that is two, three, four, five, etc. up to the king. Once a card has been correctly placed in a centre pile it may not be removed in any circumstances.

With the single exception that a card played from stock must straightaway be replaced by turning the next card in the stock pile face up, transferring a card to a centre pile takes precedence over all other moves at every stage of the game.

ii) Bearing in mind the priority of moves to the centre piles, each player at his turn can make as many of the various legal plays open to him as he wishes before a card is turned up from his hand. However, he must not play a card from hand if the exposed card on his stock is playable anywhere. This does not mean that a card from stock must be put out immediately in preference to all other plays, only that a player who proceeds to play from hand when his turned up stock card can be played violates one of the rules of precedence.

Tableau building

i) Cards are built on the tableau piles in descending sequence and alternating colour. So a red card can be played on a black, a black on a red, and a lower card in the sequence of cards on a higher. An example might be ten of hearts on the jack of spades, nine of clubs on the ten, eight of diamonds on the nine, seven of spades on the eight, and so on.

ii) Subject to the rules of precedence, cards from the stock, from other tableau piles, and from hand are all available to be used in tableau building, but under modern rules a player may not use cards from the opponent's stock for this purpose.

iii) Only the top card in a tableau pile may be moved and it is not permitted to transfer more than one card at a time. However, when possible, a card at the top of one tableau pile may be moved to the top of another in order to facilitate other moves. The cards in each tableau pile are placed neatly on top of one another and may not be looked through by the players.

iv) Moves within the tableau are not compulsory, but are made at each player's discretion.

Spaces in the tableau

i) Spaces occur when all the cards in a tableau pile have been transferred elsewhere. Although building within the tableau in order to create spaces is a valuable way of creating a place to get rid of unwanted cards, this like any other tableau move is not compulsory, except of course if a card can be transferred to the centre piles. However, when a space does occur it must be filled eventually either by a card from stock or by one from another tableau pile.

ii) Only when the stock pile is completely exhausted do the rules of precedence allow a card from hand to be used to fill a space, if this is preferred to using one from a tableau pile.

'Feeding' or 'loading'

i) A player can get rid of cards from his stock, the tableau piles, or from his hand (but not from the centre piles) by 'loading' or 'feeding' his opponent's stock or waste piles. Such loading involves building cards in suit and sequence but the sequence can run in either direction. For example the six of spades may be fed to the seven of spades, or the seven of spades to the six. If the seven is built on the six, an eight or another six can be added to the seven, and so on.

ii) Players may not load cards onto their own stock or waste piles.

Playing from hand

i) Eventually a player will exhaust all possible plays within the layout and cannot feed any cards to his opponent. Providing his exposed stock card is not playable anywhere in the layout or on his opponent's stock or waste piles, he next turns up a card from hand. This must be revealed in such a way as to give his opponent first sight of it. The new card is played immediately if a place can be found for it. Subject as always to the rules of precedence, any further plays which have been created may be made before another card is turned from hand.

ii) Once a card taken from hand has been discarded onto the waste pile because no play seems possible, the player's turn is at an end and the play passes to the opponent. Note that a player who immediately throws a card from hand into the waste pile when in fact it was playable, is often guilty only of poor play. He does not violate the rules of precedence unless the card in question could have been placed on one of the centre piles.

Waste pile

i) Cards in the waste pile are placed neatly on top of each other and the last card in it is not available for play at the next turn. This applies even if it could subsequently be added to a centre pile. It is a dead card with the sole exception that the opponent may load cards onto it.

ii) Players are not permitted to look through the waste pile, but once all the unplayed cards in the hand have been transferred to it, thereby exhausting the hand, it is immediately turned over without being shuffled, and now face down, becomes a new hand.

The 'Stop!' Rule

i) If a player thinks his opponent has violated one of the rules of precedence or any of the other rules of play, he may call, 'Stop!' The players then discuss the alleged violation and if proved, the offender immediately loses his turn.

ii) In some circles a player breaks a rule of precedence if he so much as touches one card when he should have played another, but in a friendly game the stop rule is only enforced when a player actually picks up a card and plays it illegally.

iii) After an offender's turn ends because of a violation of the rules, his opponent may let the incorrect play stand or he may require that the offending card be returned to its original position. If it was a play from the stock and is allowed to stand, the offender at once turns up a new stock card before the opponent goes on with play.

The players continue to take alternate turns after each discard onto the waste pile until one player succeeds in getting rid of all his cards into the centre and tableau piles, and by any loading. The winner scores 2 points, for each card left in the opponent's stock, and an additional 1 point for every card the opponent still has in his hand and waste pile. He also scores a 30-point bonus for winning the deal.

If neither player is able to get rid of all his cards, the player with the lowest count on the basis of 2 points for stock cards and 1 point for cards in the hand and waste pile is the winner, but he receives no bonus. Some players however prefer to declare such stalemates a draw.

A GAME IN PROGRESS

Because it always involves a very large number of moves for both players, it is not possible to show the whole of a game of Russian Bank. Below however is a hand in progress where Mary is playing Bill. The moves which Mary makes illustrate the fundamental principles of the game.

Cards beyond the top card in a pile are shown in the illustration to enable the reader to follow the commentary. In an actual game of course these would be hidden from view until turned up at the appropriate point in play.

Bill has just completed his turn by discarding the eight of clubs into his waste pile. Mary begins hers. She must make any possible plays to the centre piles before she does anything else. Accordingly she moves the three of diamonds from her stock onto the two of diamonds in the centre. Then she turns up her own two of diamonds as her new stock card and puts it at the top of the stock pile. Next she feeds the seven of clubs from the tableau onto the eight of clubs in Bill's waste, thereby creating a space. She is in no hurry to fill it and plays the two of diamonds from her stock to the three of clubs in the tableau. Her new stock card is the jack of spades. This she loads on the ten of spades in Bill's stock. She turns up the nine of hearts from her own stock and it straightaway goes on one of the two tens of clubs in the tableau. The four of hearts is her next stock card and since no other moves are possible, she uses it to fill the space she created earlier. The seven of hearts is exposed at the top of her stock. This is unplayable anywhere and she can do no more in the tableau. She has no alternative but to turn up a card from hand. It is the four of clubs. It must go immediately onto the three of clubs in the centre pile. Her stock card, the seven of hearts, still cannot be played, so again she draws a card from her hand. This is the king of clubs for which no place is available. She discards it onto her waste pile and her turn is at an end.

The new position as Bill begins his next turn is shown opposite.

HINTS ON PLAY

There are no easily formulated principles of sound play at Russian Bank, but a good player always has the edge over a lesser one. The key to the game is alertness. It is vital never to miss an opportunity of reducing cards in stock and hand by making the best use of all possible moves in the tableau and of any chances to feed the opponent. An infringement of the rules of precedence can prove very costly.

As the play proceeds the best Russian Bank exponents make a point of memorising the cards in the waste piles and the rank and suit of those hidden in the tableau piles. In this way they gain an advantage when there is a choice of moves, but it takes a great deal of practice to capitalise on such scrupulous attention to detail and it is not necessary for a full enjoyment of a game where luck plays a big part.

As an alternative to more serious card games, Russian Bank is an rewarding pastime. Although concentration is required to play well, the game can provide many hours of relaxation. It is not difficult to understand why it is one of the most popular of all family games in the U.S.A.

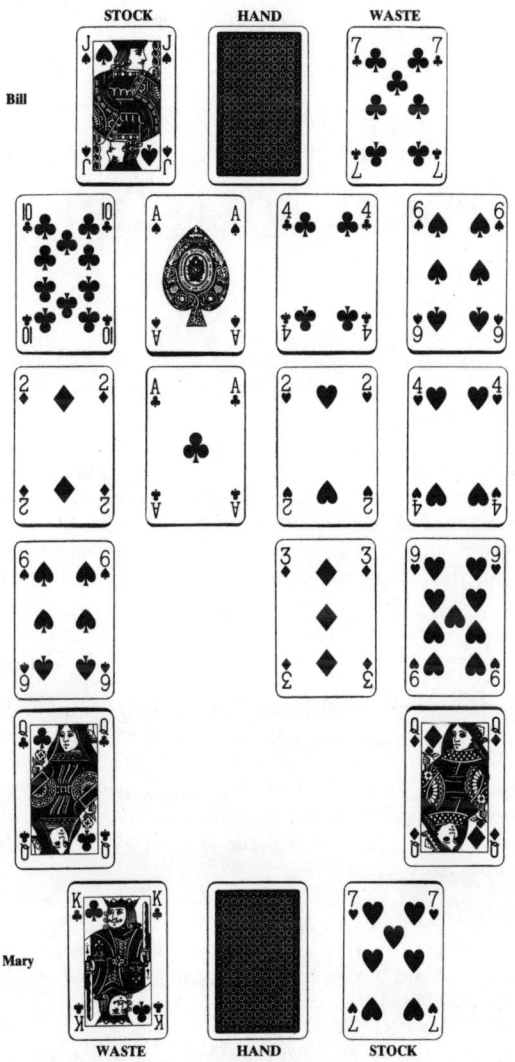

POKER SOLITAIRE

In most patiences the player either does or does not succeed in getting his game 'out' by converting shuffled cards into some ordered pattern of rank and suit according to the rules. Poker Solitaire is quite different in that the object is to score points from the 'tableau' formed during the game. It can therefore be played simply as a solitaire in which the aim is to achieve as many points as possible from each deal, or it can readily be turned into a competitive game for two or more players. It offers the opportunity to combine calculations of mathematical probability with the inspired guesses and good fortune that will result in a really handsome score. At the same time a number of preconceived strategies can be employed.

HOW TO PLAY

The idea is to lay out twenty-five cards in a square of five horizontal and five vertical rows. The cards are dealt singly and the player tries to place them in such a way that at the end of the game each row forms the best possible Poker hand. The ten resulting hands are scored individually according to their scarcity and the points from each are then added together to arrive at a final total for the tableau.
The Poker hands are:

  Straight flush: five cards of the same suit in sequence, for example seven, six, five, four, three of hearts or queen, jack, ten, nine, eight of clubs. The highest hand of this type is ace, king, queen, jack, ten of a suit and is called a **royal flush**.

  Four of a Kind: any four cards of the same rank, for example four aces, four jacks, four twos, etc.

  Straight: any five cards in sequence but not all of the same suit, for example ten of spades, nine of clubs, eight of clubs, seven of spades, six of hearts.

Full house: three of a kind and a pair, for example three aces and two eights or three sevens and two fours, and so on.

Three of a kind: three cards of the same rank and two unmatched cards, such as queen of spades, queen of clubs, queen of diamonds with say, four of hearts and three of diamonds.

Flush: any five cards of the same suit, for example king, ten, seven, four, three of spades.

Two pairs: two cards of any one rank with two cards of any other rank, and one unmatched card, for example ten of spades and ten of clubs, five of hearts and five of clubs, with ace of spades.

Pair: any two cards of the same rank with three unmatched cards, for example eight of spades and eight of diamonds with four of diamonds, five of clubs and nine of clubs.

High card: five unmatched cards which do not form any of the above hands where ace is high and two is low.

The standard fifty-two card deck without a joker is used. The order of the cards is: ace, king, queen, jack, ten, nine, eight, seven, six, five, four, three, two. However, an ace can follow a two in straight flushes and straights. The lowest hand, that is five unmatched cards, is not scored in the patience and the system of values for the other hands is slightly different to that of regular Poker because the mathematics for a twenty-five card layout are not the same as for the five cards per hand Poker game. The solitaire hands are counted:

Straight flush (including a royal flush)	30
Four of a kind	16
Straight	12
Full house	10
Three of a kind	6
Flush	5
Two pairs	3
Pair	1

As the cards are dealt out they may be positioned anywhere within the intended five by five tableau, although some players insist that each new card must be placed adjacent horizontally, vertically or diagonally to some card already played. This makes a high score much more difficult to achieve. By contrast others allow themselves a number of discards, say three or five, which may be taken at any time. So if three discards are permitted, twenty-eight cards are dealt in all and a player may throw any three away without having to use them in the tableau.

In a competitive game each player is provided with his own deck of fifty-two cards. One player is appointed dealer and the others sort their cards into numerical sequence by suit, so that any card can be located quickly. After his pack has been shuffled and cut, the dealer turns up one card at a time and calls out its rank and suit for the benefit of the rest. So the dealer forms his tableau in the normal way, but his opponents must first take out the appropriate card from their respective packs before playing it to their own layouts. At the end of a deal the layouts are counted and compared, and the player with the highest score wins. A full game may be settled over a number of deals or by one player being the first to reach some previously agreed total. 500 up for example would make a good contest.

SOME COMPLETED POKER SOLITAIRE DEALS

I

This scores on the horizontal rows, from the top, as follows:
Five unmatched cards	0	
Straight	12	
Straight	12	
Straight	12	
Straight flush	30	66

and on the vertical rows from left to right:
Pair	1	
Three of a kind	6	
Two pairs	3	
Full house	10	
Three of a kind	6	26
		92

2

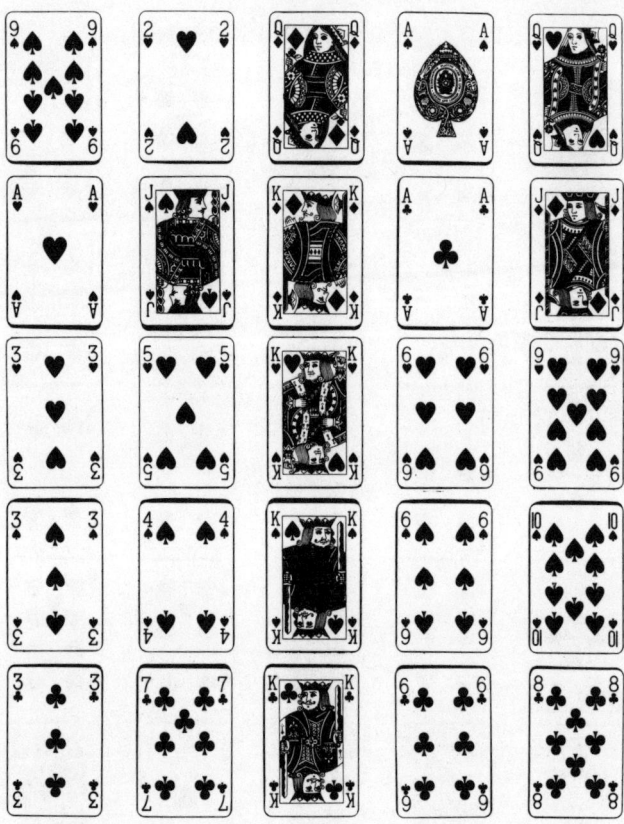

Here the scores are across, from the top:

Pair	1	
Two pairs	3	
Flush	5	
Flush	5	
Flush	<u>5</u>	19

and down, from the left:

Three of a kind	6	
Five unmatched cards	0	
Four of a kind	16	
Full house	10	
Straight	<u>12</u>	44
		<u>63</u>

This tableau would score across, from the top:

Straight	12	
Straight	12	
Five unmatched cards	0	
Pair	1	
Four of a kind	<u>16</u>	41

and on the vertical rows, left to right:

Straight flush	30	
Four of a kind	16	
Full house	10	
Five unmatched cards	0	
Two pairs	<u>3</u>	<u>59</u>
		<u>100</u>

HINTS ON PLAY

Even when not hampered by the optional rule that one card must be played so as to touch a previous one, inexperienced players tend to start by positioning a single card in relation to another single card without reference to any overall plan for how the completed tableau will eventually look. Nine times out of ten this will produce a poor score, for what usually happens is that the horizontal rows very soon begin to conflict with the vertical, and individual cards which ideally should form part of two scoring combinations, one across and one down, in fact score only once or not at all.

There are really two strategies for a good score and both are based on forward planning. They need to be adapted to circumstances, especially near the end of a deal, but they are infinitely better than *ad hoc* play which looks no further than the card actually being placed in the layout.

Flushes are easy to make, and one plan is to get them along the horizontal rows, whilst aiming for fours of a kind and full houses on the vertical. On most deals three flushes are almost certain, with several high scoring combinations possible from the downward columns. Even if the big hands fail to materialise, near misses in the shape of three of a kind and two pairs still provide the valuable consolations of 6 points and 3 points respectively.

The other standard play is riskier but will produce a very high score when it does come off. Again fours and full houses are the aim downwards but this time players try to make straights on the rows across. Straights are worth 12 compared with only 5 for a flush but they are much more difficult to achieve.

Within these two basic strategies there will be plenty of chances to assess the very best place for a particular card. There are no simple formulas for success and the art of the game lies in finding the spot which allows for the biggest margin of error in the event of things not working out exactly to plan, as so often happens.

For anyone who finds most Patiences rather repetitive, Poker Solitaire offers an unusual challenge where relative success or failure can be measured by a points score. The regular player can derive immense satisfaction from making a spectacular total on a deal, especially when this is achieved in competition with others.